Disorders, Diseases,
and Treatments

A STUDENT'S GUIDE TO

Mental Health & Wellness

VOLUME 4

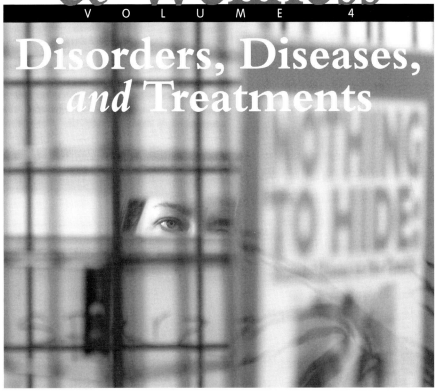

Disorders, Diseases, and Treatments

GREENWOOD PRESS
Westport, Connecticut · London

Library of Congress Cataloging-in-Publication Data

A student's guide to mental health & wellness / by Creative Media Applications.
     p. cm.
   Includes bibliographical references and index.
   Contents: v. 1. Words and terms — v. 2. Important people — v. 3. Debatable issues —
v. 4. Disorders, diseases, and treatments.
   ISBN 0–313–32548–0 (set: alk. paper) — ISBN 0–313–32549–9 (vol. 1: alk. paper) —
ISBN 0–313–32550–2 (vol. 2: alk. paper) — ISBN 0–313–32551–0 (vol. 3: alk. paper) —
ISBN 0-313-32552-9 (vol. 4: alk. paper)
     1. Mental health. 2. Health. I. Creative Media Applications.
   RA790.8.S83   2004
   616.89'0071—dc21   2003044817

British Library Cataloguing in Publication Data is available.

Library of Congress Catalog Card Number: 2003044817
ISBN: 0–313–32548–0 (set)
        0–313–32549–9 (Vol. 1)
        0–313–32550–2 (Vol. 2)
        0–313–32551–0 (Vol. 3)
        0–313–32552–9 (Vol. 4)

First published in 2004

Greenwood Press, 88 Post Road West, Westport, CT 06881
An imprint of Greenwood Publishing Group, Inc.
www.greenwood.com

Printed in the United States of America

The paper used in this book complies with the
Permanent Paper Standard issued by the National
Information Standards Organization (Z39.48–1984).

10   9   8   7   6   5   4   3   2   1

A Creative Media Applications, Inc. Production
WRITER: Robin Doak
DESIGN AND PRODUCTION: Alan Barnett, Inc.
EDITOR: Matt Levine
COPYEDITOR: Laurie Lieb
PROOFREADER: Laura Walsh
INDEXER: Nara Wood
ASSOCIATED PRESS PHOTO RESEARCHER: Yvette Reyes
CONSULTANT: John Rickards, Professor of Psychology, University of Connecticut at Storrs

PHOTO CREDITS:
Cover: AP/Wide World Photographs
© CORBIS *page:* viii
© Hulton Archives/Getty Images *pages:* 5, 123, 125, 126
AP/Wide World Photographs *pages:* iii, 7, 8, 12, 15, 26, 29, 38, 42, 46, 51, 53, 57, 60, 65, 69, 73, 81, 82,
   87, 95, 99, 107, 112, 120, 127
© Pete Saloutos/CORBIS *page:* 17
© Tom Stewart/CORBIS *page:* 20
© Tom & Dee Ann McCarthy/CORBIS *page:* 35
© K.BeebeCustom Medical Stock Photo *page:* 77
© David Woods/CORBIS *page:* 90
© David Pollack/CORBIS *page:* 102
© Bettmann/CORBIS *page:* 124

jR616.89 STUDENTS v.4
A student's guide to mental
health & wellness

Table of Contents

This book is intended to provide you with information about psychological disorders. However, it does not provide professional advice, and it is not intended to be used to diagnose psychological or mental health problems. If you have any concerns about mental health issues, please discuss them with your parents or school counselors, or consult a qualified health care professional in your community.

Introduction

Good mental health is a key part of overall wellness. It is as important to stay in top shape emotionally and intellectually as it is to be physically fit. In fact, mental wellness can contribute to good physical health.

It is important for everyone to be aware of mental health issues. One way people can stay mentally healthy is to develop a good understanding of how the mind works. Knowing how stress, disease, and other factors affect mental health can help people better maintain their mental wellness. It's also important to know the warning signs of a more serious mental health problem that may require the assistance of a mental health professional.

Today, the importance of staying mentally healthy is well known and documented. Like physical ailments and conditions, mental health issues should be taken seriously and addressed. Thousands of people work in fields that help people maintain mental health. These fields include social work, psychology, and psychiatry. A basic knowledge of psychology is also important in many other fields, including teaching, law enforcement, and crisis counseling.

Mental Health and Psychology

Mental health and wellness are both part of a larger science called *psychology*. Psychology is the scientific study of how people think, feel, and behave. For centuries, humans have tried to explain the workings of the mind. Some of the first people to try to understand the brain and its effect on human behavior were the ancient Greeks. The theories and ideas of Greek philosophers and physicians laid the groundwork for the study of psychology.

Despite advances in understanding mental health, stigmas against people with mental illness have persisted through the centuries. In colonial times, mentally ill people were usually viewed as evil or corrupt. Many were locked away for the duration of their lives. Only in recent times have we come to understand that mental illnesses, in most cases, can be treated effectively with medicines and therapy.

Today, there is still much to be learned about psychology and mental wellness. Researchers continue to study the brain and how it works. Thanks to technological advances, they can even take pictures of the human brain in action. Another important area of study is the search for causes of mental illnesses. Understanding why some people develop mental disorders can help doctors develop more effective ways to prevent, treat, and even cure these conditions.

George III was king of England from 1760 to 1820. Most famous for ruling during the American Revolution (1775–1783), later in life he suffered from mental illness. Because he was royalty, however, he did not have to endure the usual fate of the mentally ill of his time.

Overview of This Series

A Student's Guide to Mental Health & Wellness is a four-volume series designed as an introduction to psychology. It shows how the study of this important field can be applied to the issues in our daily lives.

The first volume, *Words and Terms,* introduces words and phrases used throughout the rest of the series. Here are definitions of such terms as *mental disorders, anorexia nervosa,* and *cognitive psychology.* Volume 1 includes a "Connections" section for each term, to show how it fits into the science of psychology.

The second volume, *Important People,* describes the men and women who have pioneered the science of psychology and advanced the knowledge of mental health and wellness. The volume also offers a brief history of psychology as well as an overview of the types of psychotherapy and research methods.

Volume 3, *Debatable Issues,* provides the facts behind some hot topics in the news today. Standardized testing, the effect of media violence on children, and other current events related to psychology are covered with pro and con views at the beginning of each piece.

The final volume of the series, *Disorders, Diseases, and Treatments,* covers the most commonly diagnosed mental illnesses. The volume includes symptoms and effects of each disease, along with diagnosis and treatment information. It also includes tips on how to stay as mentally healthy as possible.

Pronunciation

You will notice that in the pronunciation guides, the words are not broken into syllables. Rather, they are sectioned off by the way that they sound so you can figure out how to say them. The piece of each word in CAPITAL LETTERS is where you put the emphasis. That means it is the part you pronounce slightly louder.

Note: All metric conversions in this book are approximate.

CHAPTER 1
Mental Disorders

The brain is the body's control center. It regulates our thoughts, emotions, behaviors, and mental health. Over the years, researchers have learned more and more about this important organ, yet many mysteries still surround the brain and its workings.

Many of these mysteries concern mental illness. *Mental illness* is a general term for any and all mental disorders. A *mental disorder* is an abnormality in thought, emotion, mood, or behavior in which a cluster of symptoms persists and causes disability or discomfort. Mental disorders, whether mild or severe, can interfere with a person's ability to handle the normal, daily activities of life that most people take for granted.

What Causes Mental Illness?

Mental illnesses are more common than you may think. According to recent studies, as many as one out of every five Americans suffers from a mental illness during any given year. Mental illness becomes a serious health issue when the symptoms are severe and *chronic,* or long-lasting, or if the condition affects a person's ability to lead a normal, fulfilling life.

There is still much to be learned about what causes many types of mental health disorders. Current research has indicated, however, that mental health disorders probably result from a combination of genetic and environmental factors.

People of all ages, races, and economic levels can be affected by mental health conditions. However, some people are more likely than others to develop these disorders. That's because they have a *genetic predisposition* for certain conditions. This means that these conditions seem to run in their family from generation to generation.

Some mental health disorders are more strongly linked to genetic influences than others are. Such disorders include autism and some other pervasive developmental disorders, schizophrenia, bipolar disorder, and attention deficit hyperactivity disorder (ADHD).

Environmental risk factors for developing a mental health disorder can be found at home, at school, or in the community. Some of the many environmental risk factors include having a mother who drank alcohol, used illegal drugs, or smoked while pregnant; poverty; child abuse; having a parent with a mental health disorder or other problems; and a traumatic event.

It is impossible to tell how much impact an environmental factor will have on any one person. It depends upon the person's age, the person's resilience (ree-ZIL-yense), the severity of the event, and whether the factor occurred by itself or with other events. The same factor may affect two different people in two different ways.

Mental health professionals and researchers continue to look for more information about the causes of mental illness. A better understanding of what causes these serious conditions will hopefully lead to more effective treatments, as well as preventive measures.

Fast Fact

Doctors know that mental health and physical health are closely related. Mental disorders can lead to physical ailments and diseases. Physical changes in the brain or other physical health problems may affect mental health or cause mental illness.

Mental Health and Children

Mental health conditions are not uncommon in children. A 1999 study estimated that nearly 21 percent of children between the ages of nine and seventeen suffered from a diagnosable (dye-ag-NOH-suh-bul) mental health disorder. Mental health conditions can also affect younger children.

There are a number of warning signs that indicate that a child or adolescent (ad-uh-LESS-ent) may have a mental health problem. These signs include poor performance in school, sudden loss of interest in normally enjoyed activities, unexplained fears, long-lasting sleep problems, and an obsession with or loss of interest in appearance.

However, mental health professionals warn that caution should be used when diagnosing (dye-ag-NOH-sing) children. Children are still growing. Some of the "symptoms" of a mental health disorder might really be appropriate behavior for a particular age group. For example, toddlers are naturally restless and fidgety. Adolescents normally experience changes in moods. Major events, such as a death in the family, divorce, or moving, can affect a child's emotions and mental wellness at any age. Only when normal emotions and behaviors become so severe that they interfere with the child's relationships with family and peers, occur consistently over a long period of time, or cause disability do professionals worry that a mental illness may exist.

Warning Signs

There are a number of warning signs of a mental health disorder. In children and adolescents, symptoms to watch for include the following:

• Changes in appetite or eating behavior over an extended period of time

• Withdrawal from friends and family

• Sudden fearfulness

• Self-destructive behavior or frequent injuries

• Behavior that regresses to an earlier stage of development (for example, bed-wetting or sucking the thumb)

If the behaviors persist or cause problems in the child's daily life, professional help should be sought.

Mental Health Care in the Past

Mental illnesses are real and serious health conditions that can be treated with professional help. Today, most people understand that patients suffering from mental health disorders—like those suffering from cancer or heart disease—are not to blame for their conditions. However, it wasn't always this way.

In the past, people with mental illness were blamed for their own sickness. In early colonial America, for example, mentally ill people were considered wicked or possessed by the devil. They were usually locked away for the duration of their lives. In some places, people who were probably suffering from mental health conditions were accused of witchcraft and sentenced to death.

In the early 1800s, a handful of *asylums* (uh-SYE-lumz), or hospitals, for the mentally ill sprang up. Here, patients were locked up and given mostly experimental treatments. These treatments ranged from the useless to the life-threatening. Adults were not the only people confined in these mental hospitals. Children with many types of mental health conditions, viewed as untreatable, were also placed in these institutions. For example, children with autism were institutionalized for their entire lives.

The 1940s and 1950s saw an effort to reform hospitals for the mentally ill. This reform included *deinstitutionalization* (dee-in-stih-too-shun-ul-ih-ZAY-shun), the effort to take most mentally ill people out of the hospitals and help them become productive, functioning members of society. This effort was greatly helped by the development of the earliest drugs to treat schizophrenia and other mental illnesses. During the 1970s and 1980s, thousands of mentally ill people were released from institutions. Some returned to their families, others went to nursing homes and boardinghouses, and still others were released with nowhere to go and no real support to help them adjust and thrive in the outside world. Today, there is still a serious debate about the effectiveness of deinstitutionalization.

In recent years, the most common mode of mental health treatment has become short-term stays in the hospital, with the family and community involved in a patient's long-term care.

The Pennsylvania Hospital and Benjamin Rush

One of the first hospitals to treat the mentally ill was the Pennsylvania Hospital in Philadelphia, Pennsylvania. Opened in 1752, the hospital had a special, separate wing for people suffering from mental health conditions. At first, mental patients were treated as cruelly here as they were anywhere else, being chained to the walls in dark cells.

In the 1780s, physician Benjamin Rush (1745–1813) greatly improved the conditions for the mentally ill at the Pennsylvania Hospital. Rush separated the most violent patients from the other patients. He also made sure that all mental patients had heat and fresh air in their rooms. Rush instituted programs that allowed the patients to work, exercise, and do other activities.

Dr. Benjamin Rush was one of the first people to make an effort to improve conditions for mentally ill patients in a hospital. He worked at the Pennsylvania Hospital in Philadelphia in the late eighteenth century.

Mental Health Care Today

In recent years, efforts to better understand and treat mental illness have been made throughout the United States. In 1999, the surgeon general released the first report on mental health in the United States. Research continues, and mental health campaigns bring awareness and knowledge to the American public.

As new medical technologies are developed and scientists learn more about the brain, researchers are better able to formulate effective treatments for people with mental health conditions. One focus for mental health researchers is finding ways to prevent mental illnesses before they occur. Researchers are also attempting to discover what causes certain mental disorders. The causes of most mental health conditions remain unknown.

Health professionals have also begun focusing on mental health disorders that have their onset during childhood and adolescence. It has been shown that adults who suffer from mental health problems often had related problems as children. If mental health disorders can be identified and diagnosed early, the chances of effectively treating these conditions improve.

Although treatment of mental disorders is more effective than ever, nearly two-thirds of all Americans with diagnosable mental illnesses are not currently seeking treatment. Researchers believe that one reason is that many people cannot afford treatment. Currently, an important focus for local, state, and national policy makers interested in mental health care is to ensure that treatment for these serious conditions is accessible to all people, regardless of income. Currently, underinsured or uninsured people and those with low income have little or no access to good mental health care.

Another reason that people do not seek out mental health care is the fear of being stigmatized. A stigma is a mark of disgrace or shame. Although people today know more about mental illnesses than ever before, some people's views of the mentally ill remain stuck in the past. A 1996 survey of Americans showed that stigmas against the seriously ill still linger.

Each May, mental health professionals work to break down the stigmas surrounding mental illness during Mental Health Month. It's important for all people suffering from mental health conditions to understand that they are not alone and that they can get help. People who do not receive treatment for their mental illnesses may experience a much lower quality of life, including problems at work, at home, and in the community.

Famous People and Mental Health Conditions

Throughout history, many well-known people have suffered from conditions that affected their mental health.

Ludwig van Beethoven (1770–1827), the German composer, was known in his time for his mood swings, as well as for his brilliant musical compositions. Today, some biographers believe that Beethoven suffered from bipolar disorder.

Winston Churchill (1874–1965), the prime minister of Great Britain during World War II (1939–1945), suffered from frequent episodes of major depression and bipolar disorder throughout his life.

Abraham Lincoln (1809–1865), the sixteenth president of the United States, battled major depression, including suicidal (soo-ih-SYDE-ul) thoughts, throughout his life.

John Nash (1928–), a mathematical genius, has been plagued by schizophrenia for much of his life. His struggle with this mental illness was featured in the 2001 movie, *A Beautiful Mind*.

Virginia Woolf (1882–1941), the respected British author, wrote *To the Lighthouse* and *Orlando*. She also suffered from bipolar disorder. Woolf eventually committed suicide because she could no longer bear the disorder.

Keeping It Confidential

Many people refuse to seek treatment for a mental disorder because they fear that others will learn of their problem and treat them differently. For this reason, it is important that mental health workers keep treatment confidential. The U.S. Supreme Court has ruled that the relationship between a person and his or her therapist is confidential and cannot be disclosed.

CHAPTER 2
Mood Disorders

Mood disorders affect the way that a person feels. Mood disorders can cause a person to feel extremely sad and lethargic or elated and energetic. They can affect a person's energy levels, appetite, interests, and ability to function normally.

According to the National Institute of Mental Health (NIMH), nearly 19 million Americans suffer from a mood disorder during any given year. The three main types of mood disorders are major depression, dysthymia, and bipolar disorder.

Major Depression

Bad things happen to everyone. Divorce, the loss of a loved one, the breakup of a friendship—even a failed test can cause unhappiness. It's natural to feel sad or "blue" when these events interrupt the normal flow of life.

Feelings of sadness become a problem when they last longer than two weeks or interfere with a person's ability to function for an extended period of time. When this happens, a person is suffering from a serious medical condition known as *major depression* (dih-PREH-shun).

According to the World Health Organization (WHO), major depression is the number one cause of disability in the United States and the world today. The disorder affects about 9.5 percent of all American adults during any given year.

What Is Major Depression?

Major depression can alter a person's mood and thoughts, interfering with the ability to work, learn, and lead a normal, productive life. Major depression can also affect a person's physical well-being by altering eating and sleeping habits.

Symptoms of depression include the following:

- Feelings of sadness, emptiness, or anxiety that persist over time
- Feelings of hopelessness, worthlessness, and guilt
- Loss of interest in and enjoyment of activities that were once fun
- Loss of energy
- Problems concentrating, remembering, and making decisions
- Oversleeping or difficulty sleeping
- Changes in appetite and weight
- Thoughts of death and suicide; attempted suicide
- Restlessness or irritability
- Headaches, stomach pains, aching joints and muscles, or other physical ailments that do not respond to treatment

What Causes Depression?

Some researchers believe that chemical imbalances in the brain can lead to depression. In recent years, researchers have worked to figure out why some people develop these chemical imbalances while others do not. They believe that some people are genetically predisposed to develop the condition. That's because major depression tends to run in some families, passed on from generation to generation.

Depression triggers include physical conditions and physical changes. Parkinson's disease, heart attacks, cancer, and glandular problems, for example, have all been shown to trigger major depression in some people. This can cause serious problems, because the patient is less likely to seek out proper medical attention.

A major depression may also be triggered by a specific, traumatic event. The death of a close relative, a divorce, or moving to a new home can all trigger depression in people who may be genetically predisposed to the condition.

Women and Depression

Women are twice as likely as men to suffer from depression. According to the NIMH, one out of every four women and one out of every eight men will suffer from depression at some point in their lives. Women are also more likely to seek help for depression than are men.

Researchers believe that hormonal factors may play an important role in causing depression in women. The hormone levels in a woman's body change during the menstrual cycle, as well as during and after pregnancy. Environmental stresses are another factor that may trigger depression in some women.

One type of depression that may be brought about by hormonal changes is *premenstrual* (pree-MEN-stroo-ul) *syndrome* (PMS), also known as premenstrual dysphoria (diss-FOR-ee-uh). This type of depression begins between five and eleven days before a woman's menstrual cycle and lasts until the woman begins menstruating.

Many women with PMS find that their symptoms ease when they make some changes in their daily habits, such as exercising regularly; eating a healthy diet; avoiding caffeine, salt, and alcohol; and getting plenty of rest. Such painkillers as aspirin and ibuprofen can relieve physical symptoms associated with PMS. In more serious cases, doctors may prescribe other medication and therapy (THERR-uh-pee) to help patients find relief.

Another type of depression that affects women is known as *postpartum* (poste-PART-um) *depression,* which occurs after childbirth. While many new mothers experience mild feelings of sadness after the birth of a child, other women may develop serious depression. A few women also develop psychotic symptoms, including hallucinations (huh-loo-sih-NAY-shunz) and delusions (deh-LOO-zhunz). Postpartum depression, which usually develops within the first four weeks after birth, affects about 1 percent of all new mothers. Like PMS, the condition may be caused by hormonal and physical changes.

Symptoms of PMS

Premenstrual syndrome causes both physical and emotional symptoms. These symptoms include the following:

Physical	Emotional
Bloating	Anxiety
Headaches	Difficulty concentrating
Backaches	Depression
Swollen ankles, feet, or hands	Irritability
Abdominal cramps, pain, or swelling	Confusion
Breast tenderness	Forgetfulness
Weight gain	Low self-esteem
Cold sores	Paranoia
Acne problems	Poor judgment
Nausea	Feelings of guilt
Food cravings	Fatigue

Regular exercise, including yoga (the stretching exercise shown here), is good for overall health and well-being, and it also relieves some of the symptoms of PMS, both physical and emotional.

Children and Depression

Depression is a mental health condition that affects people of all ages. According to the NIMH, between 3 and 5 percent of all adolescents experience serious depression each year. On average, these episodes of depression last between seven and nine months. Although depression most commonly occurs for the first time between the ages of fifteen and thirty, the condition can also affect younger children.

Some children are at a higher risk for depression than others. Adolescent girls are twice as likely to develop depression as boys are. Some researchers believe that this is because girls are more socially oriented than boys and become more upset and stressed-out as a result of peer problems. Other studies have indicated that girls' coping mechanisms may play a part. Girls tend to dwell on a problem or adverse event, while boys tend to put the problem out of their minds. This can sometimes be bad for boys if ignoring the problem later leads to aggressive behavior. Other risk factors include the following:

• A history of child abuse

• The death of a parent

• A divorce

• A chronic illness

• A family history of depression

• The breakup of a romantic relationship

• Stress

• A natural disaster or other trauma

• Cigarette smoking

Diagnosing depression in a child or teen can be difficult. In many cases, the condition is mistaken for another problem or the normal mood changes that go along with growing up. Parents and teachers may believe that the child is just moody or "going through a phase."

Every child and adolescent experiences some of these symptoms from time to time. There is only cause for concern when sad feelings and other symptoms persist over an extended period of time. Symptoms of depression in a child or teen include the following:

- Reluctance to attend school
- A sudden drop in grades
- Reckless behavior, such as using alcohol or drugs or engaging in unsafe sexual intercourse
- Irritability or hostile, aggressive behavior (shouting, complaining, crying, fighting)
- Problems with friends or family (including running away)
- Self-criticism or feelings of being criticized by others
- Neglect of appearance and hygiene
- Disturbance of sleeping patterns

One serious symptom of depression in teens and children is an obsession with death and dying. Children with depression may have suicidal thoughts or an excessive fear of death. These thoughts and feelings should be taken seriously.

Reactive Depression Affects Everyone

The most common mood disorder experienced by children and adolescents is called *reactive depression*. Reactive depression is short-lived depressed feelings that occur as a result of a minor, unhappy experience. A failed test or a broken toy may cause someone to suffer reactive depression, for example. Usually the person's mood soon improves, especially when something good occurs in the person's life. Reactive depression is not considered a mental health disorder.

Effects of Depression

Major depression can affect more than just the mind. Depression can also lead to physical problems. Recent research has shown that the condition increases the risk of suffering coronary heart disease.

Sometimes, people with major depression try to make themselves feel better or ease their pain. Substance abuse, especially among men, is a serious complication of depression. Some researchers believe that depressed people may use alcohol and other drugs to "self-medicate," or ease their own pain without professional help.

Suicide

One of the most serious effects of major depression is suicide. *Suicide* (SOO-ih-syde) is the act of deliberately killing oneself. Not everyone who has depression attempts suicide, but the fact remains that people suffering from major depression are more

Suicide is a devastating result of the effects of depression in some people. It affects many young people—in 2000, it was the third leading cause of death of people aged ten to twenty-four. These California teens mourn the suicide of two friends.

likely to try to kill themselves than people who are not suffering from depression. According to the National Institutes of Health (NIH), 10 percent of all people who threaten or attempt suicide eventually do kill themselves.

Suicide is an especially serious problem among young people in the United States. In 2000, suicide was the third leading cause of death among Americans aged ten to twenty-four. (Accidents and homicide were the top two.) Additionally, there is strong evidence to indicate that 90 percent of all children and adolescents who actually committed suicide had some sort of mental health disorder.

The risk of suicide is greatest among adolescents who suffer from major depression. Studies have shown that as many as 7 percent of all adolescents with major depression commit suicide in their young adult years. The risk of suicide among depressed children and teens increases even more if the child also has a conduct disorder or a substance abuse disorder. Unfortunately, recent research indicates that less than one-third of all suicidal teenagers seek professional help. When teenagers do seek help, most turn to school professionals or a private doctor's office.

Depression and the Elderly

Elderly people are at high risk for depression. As people age, their health and physical capabilities may deteriorate. As a result, they may lose some of their independence. In addition, elderly people are likely to have experienced the death of a loved one. These events can all trigger severe depression.

Depression is a serious problem for elderly people. Some older people with depression attempt and commit suicide. In fact, the highest rate of suicide in the United States is among the elderly.

Elderly people can be treated with medications and therapy. In severe cases, doctors may recommend electroconvulsive (ee-lek-troh-kon-VUL-siv) therapy (ECT).

A loss of independence, health, and loved ones can contribute to the serious problem of depression in the elderly. Maintaining relationships, contacts with others, and keeping occupied can protect elderly people from depression.

Recognizing Suicide Risk

There are a number of signs that indicate that a person might be thinking about suicide. According to the NIH, the following are warning signs:

• Withdrawal and isolation

• Moodiness

• Personality changes

• Threats of suicide

• Giving away cherished possessions or tidying up and putting things in order

If a friend is talking about suicide, here are some tips on what to do:

• Take your friend seriously.

- Don't try to deal with the problem alone—seek help immediately. Call your friend's doctor, the local emergency room, or 911. The person needs to be evaluated immediately by a professional.
- Don't leave your friend alone.
- Make sure that your friend does not have access to any weapons or other means of harm.
- Let your friend know how important he or she is to you.

If a friend or loved one does commit suicide, those left behind often feel angry or blame themselves. It's important for survivors to seek help and support for themselves and to remember that they are not at fault.

Self-Injury

Another effect of major depression may be self-injury. *Self-injury* is the deliberate harming of oneself without the intention of committing suicide. Forms of self-injury include cutting, scratching, tattooing, excessive body piercing, burning, and head banging. Although self-injury is not recognized as a mental health condition, it has become more common among adolescents in recent years. Adolescents who engage in self-injury are more likely than other adolescents to commit suicide later.

Most people who injure themselves are in their late teens, twenties, and thirties. Girls are more likely to hurt themselves than boys are. Risk factors include a childhood history of physical or sexual abuse and abnormal brain chemical levels.

People may choose to injure themselves for a variety of reasons. Some do it to rebel against authority; others use self-injury as a way to let out feelings of rage, grief, or frustration that are bottled up inside. Whatever the reason, self-injury is a condition that shouldn't be ignored. In some cases, it indicates a much more serious mental health condition, such as an eating disorder, bipolar disorder, or a substance abuse disorder.

Self-injury can lead to other health problems. Cutting can cause serious injury, require stitches, become infected, and leave behind permanent scars. Using dirty knives or needles can also lead to such diseases as hepatitis and acquired immune deficiency syndrome (AIDS).

Doctors normally treat people who injure themselves with a combination of therapy and medication. Medications include antidepressants, mood stabilizers, and antianxiety drugs. Professionals can teach patients techniques to relax and find other, more positive ways to express their feelings.

Fast Fact

Two-thirds of all people who have major depression also suffer from another mental health condition, such as dysthymia, an anxiety disorder, or a substance abuse problem. Substance abuse is often associated with depression.

Diagnosing and Treating Depression

Most Americans do not seek treatment for depression. Many believe that the bad or sad feelings are a sign of weakness. Others believe that they can handle their problems by themselves. Major depression, however, cannot be willed away. People cannot "snap out" of a depression. Without treatment, major depression can last for months or even years.

If you think that you (or someone you know) may be suffering from depression, the first thing to do is to talk to someone you trust or to seek professional help. Doctors and mental health professionals can help most people who suffer from major depression.

Major depression is usually classified as the presence of five or more of the symptoms associated with the condition. The first step in diagnosing depression is to rule out any other medical conditions. To do this, doctors will perform a complete physical examination. They will check for any illnesses or ailments that might be causing the symptoms. Lab tests may be used to rule out viral infections or other diseases.

Doctors will also need to learn the patient's complete psychological (sye-koh-LAH-jik-ul) history. They will want to know when the symptoms started, how severe the symptoms are, whether the patient has ever suffered the symptoms before or been treated for them before, and whether depression or

Gathering a thorough psychological history of a patient can help a doctor diagnose and treat depression. A physical examination is important, too, to rule out any illnesses that may be causing depression-like symptoms.

these symptoms run in the family. Medical professionals may also ask about a history of drug use or suicidal thoughts or attempts. Finally, they will evaluate whether the depression has affected the person's speech, memory, or thought patterns.

Doctors most often use psychotherapy, medication, or a combination of these two treatments to help a person with depression. For people with mild depression, psychotherapy may be used by itself. For those with more serious cases, antidepressant medication may be used along with psychotherapy.

For people with severe depression or for those who cannot take antidepressants, doctors may recommend ECT. ECT is a treatment that uses electricity to cause a brief seizure in the brain. The seizure releases brain chemicals that make the brain work better. Patients are first given a muscle relaxant and then anesthesia (an-ess-THEE-zhuh). Electrodes attached to the patient's head deliver the electric "impulse." The treatment is usually given three times a week for several weeks.

Unfortunately, it is difficult to "cure" major depression. As many as seven out of ten children and adolescents who suffer from depression will have a recurrence of the condition by the time that they are adults.

Can Herbs Cure Depression?

For hundreds of years, people have used an herb called St. John's wort as a folk remedy to treat depression and anxiety. In Europe, the herb remains a popular way to treat depression. In the United States, however, recent studies have indicated that St. John's wort is probably not an effective treatment for patients with moderate or severe major depression. Studies are still being conducted about the herb's effectiveness in milder cases of depression.

In 2000, the Food and Drug Administration (FDA) issued a warning about St. John's wort. (The FDA is the U.S. agency responsible for regulation of all food and drug products available to the public.) Although the herb is safe, it can reduce the effectiveness of other important drugs used to treat AIDS patients and organ-transplant patients.

Dysthymia

Dysthymia (diss-THYE-mee-uh) is a chronic type of depression. Although the symptoms of dysthymia are less severe than those of major depression, they can last much longer. While these symptoms do not cause complete disability, they can keep patients from enjoying life and functioning to their fullest. For many people, the first occurrence of dysthymia is in childhood or adolescence.

Symptoms of dysthymia include poor self-image and feelings of hopelessness. Other effects of the disorder include changes in eating habits and sleeping patterns, low energy, and lack of concentration. As many as 5 percent of all Americans suffer from the disorder. Women are more likely than men to develop the disorder.

Doctors diagnose dysthymia after a patient has suffered from a depressed mood along with two other symptoms of major depression for two years or longer (one year or longer for a child). Seven out of every ten people who suffer from dysthymia eventually experience major depression later in their lives.

For children and adolescents, the average duration of dysthymia is about four years. According to the 1999 surgeon general's report on mental health, some children suffer from the condition for so long that the depressed feelings seem normal to them. These children do not recognize the symptoms for what they are and do not seek help.

Researchers believe that a combination of medications and therapy provides the most effective treatment for dysthymia. Antidepressant medications can ease symptoms. Psychotherapy is useful in helping patients learn to cope with their disorder. However, it is difficult to successfully treat dysthymia in the long run. Symptoms often persist for years, despite treatment.

Seasonal Affective Disorder

Seasonal affective disorder (SAD) is a rare type of depression that begins each year at the start of fall or winter and eases in the springtime, when warm, sunny weather starts to arrive. Less sunlight contributes to the feelings of depression. According to the National Mental Health Association (NMHA), January and February are the most difficult months for SAD sufferers.

Doctors don't know what causes SAD. Some researchers believe that it may be caused by changes in body temperature or hormone regulation. Most people begin to develop the condition in late adolescence or early adulthood. Women are more likely to develop SAD than men are.

Symptoms of SAD include lack of energy, loss of interest in work and other activities, increased appetite—especially a craving for carbohydrates—and weight gain, drowsiness and an increased need for sleep, social withdrawal, and feelings of slowness or sluggishness.

People with SAD are often treated with *light therapy*—spending time under a special, bright light. As long as SAD patients continue this therapy, they usually feel much better. In serious cases, SAD can develop into major depression.

Bipolar Disorder

Bipolar (bye-POH-lur) *disorder,* also known as *manic depression,* is a type of mood disorder that causes both low and high emotions. People with bipolar disorder experience a cycle of mood changes that range from elevated moods and hyperactivity to severe sadness and withdrawal. Periods of elevated moods are known as *manic episodes,* while periods of low moods are called *depressive moods.*

More than 2 million Americans over the age of eighteen will be affected by bipolar disorder during any given year. The condition affects men and women equally. Doctors are not sure what causes bipolar disorder, but they do know that there is a strong genetic link. Many people who develop bipolar disorder have a relative who also has the condition.

A bipolar person's change in mood is usually gradual, taking place over a period of hours or days. This change from one mood to another is known as *cycling.* However, the change from mania to depression can also be sudden and extreme. In either case, these shifts in mood can interfere with a person's ability to live a normal, productive life.

A person in a depressive stage may have some or all of the symptoms of someone with a major depression. Symptoms of an adult in a manic stage include the following:

• A high level of energy and activity, including increased talking and racing thoughts

• Feelings of elation and invulnerability

• Irritability

• A decreased need for sleep

• Grandiose ideas

• Poor judgment

• Inappropriate social behavior

Many bipolar patients enjoy the manic stage. It feels good. Patients feel energized, confident, and uninhibited. If left untreated, however, mania can progress to a psychotic state. A *psychotic* (sye-KAHT-ik) state is one in which the patient completely loses touch with reality.

Diagnosing and Treating Bipolar Disorder

Before making a diagnosis (dye-ag-NOH-siss) of bipolar disorder, doctors will first perform complete physical and psychiatric (sye-kee-AT-rik) exams in order to rule out other medical conditions and to eliminate the possibility that drugs are causing the problems. Doctors need to learn how long the patient has been suffering from the symptoms of bipolar disorder and if there is a history of the condition in the patient's family. Finally, they will observe the patient to determine how serious the condition is.

The most effective treatment for bipolar disorder is a combination of medications and therapy. The most common medications given to bipolar patients are mood stabilizers, which help control mood swings. Therapy and support groups help patients and their families take control of their lives.

People suffering from severe bipolar disorder may need to be hospitalized. They will then be given antidepressant and antipsychotic medicines to stabilize their condition.

Children and Bipolar Disorder

Bipolar disorder is not just a condition that affects adults. Children and adolescents can also develop the condition. In fact, most people develop bipolar disorder between the ages of fifteen and twenty-five. Researchers believe that bipolar disorder that develops in children may be a completely different and much more severe condition than bipolar disorder that develops in adolescence or adulthood.

Children with bipolar disorder are more likely to experience continuous, rapid mood changes. During manic phases, bipolar children are likely to suffer from extreme irritability. They may also be prone to destructive behavior.

It is often difficult to diagnose bipolar disorder in young people. The symptoms of the disorder are often mistaken for the normal moods and behaviors of children at certain ages. In addition, children with bipolar disorder may also have another condition, such as ADHD or a conduct disorder. Research on bipolar disorder and children is currently being conducted.

Like major depression, bipolar disorder can lead to some serious side effects, including alcohol and drug abuse and physical ailments. People with bipolar disorder, particularly children and adolescents, may have difficulty in forming and maintaining relationships.

Cyclothymia

Cyclothymia (sye-kloh-THYE-mee-uh) is a type of chronic, mild bipolar disorder in which patients cycle from short periods of depression to short periods of mania. In a patient with this condition, mood changes occur suddenly and with little regularity. Although cyclothymia is not as serious as bipolar disorder, it can still interfere with a person's ability to function.

Cyclothymia is usually diagnosed after the patient has experienced the symptoms of the condition for two years or longer. Like bipolar disorder, most patients with cyclothymia need to undergo long-term treatment to prevent mood swings from recurring. In addition, patients with the disorder have an increased risk of developing major depression or bipolar disorder.

Blaming bipolar disorder for his behavior, this West Virginia lawyer resigned his job after being accused of unprofessional conduct, including practicing law without a license. Manic stages of bipolar disorder often cause sufferers to use poor judgment.

CHAPTER 3

Personality Disorders and Dissociative Disorders

Personality (per-sun-AL-ih-tee) *disorders* are mental health conditions that affect a person's ability to lead a happy, healthy life. A person with a personality disorder may have difficulty handling relationships and the normal stresses of day-to-day living. Researchers are not sure what causes personality disorders, but genetic and environmental factors are thought to play a part.

Treatment of a personality disorder is often difficult. Many people with these conditions do not seek treatment on their own. In addition, doctors have so far been unable to find any medication or therapy that is consistently effective. For some people, symptoms ease when they enter middle age.

Borderline Personality Disorder

Borderline personality disorder (BPD) is a mental health condition that is marked by unstable moods and impulsive behavior. BPD affects emotions, relationships, behaviors, and self-image. It can lead to problems at home, in the workplace, and in other areas as well.

Symptoms of BPD include feelings of depression, anger, or anxiety that last for a few hours or as long as a day. While experiencing these feelings, the patient might be prone to impulsive acts that include drug abuse, aggression, self-injury, or risky sexual practices. A patient with BPD often has difficulties in establishing normal relationships. The patient's feelings about a person may swing back and forth, from love and adoration to hate and disgust. The patient may also have low self-esteem and feel like a victim of circumstances. Things are usually all good or all bad.

BPD has the potential to negatively impact every aspect of a person's life. Research has shown that BPD places people at higher risk of being victims of violence, including sexual assault and other crimes.

According to the NIMH, BPD is more common than schizophrenia and bipolar disorder. As many as 2 percent of adult Americans are affected by BPD. Most of these sufferers are young women.

As with other personality disorders, both genetic and environmental elements may play a part. People who develop BPD may be genetically predisposed to not handle stress as well as other people. Many people who develop BPD have reported a childhood history of abuse, neglect, or separation. Between 40 and 71 percent of BPD patients report an incident of sexual abuse in their past.

BPD often occurs simultaneously with other mental health conditions, such as bipolar disorder, depression, anxiety disorders, eating disorders, and substance abuse disorders.

Diagnosing and Treating BPD

Mental health professionals diagnose BPD after thorough physical and psychiatric exams have been performed. A physical exam is used to rule out any other medical conditions that might be causing the problems. During the psychiatric evaluation, doctors ask questions about the patient's history. The doctors will also want to know how long the patient has been experiencing symptoms.

Research has shown that therapy is an effective way to treat some patients suffering from BPD. Group therapy may be more effective than individual therapy in some cases. For some patients with BPD, doctors prescribe medications to control certain symptoms.

Dialectical behavior therapy (DBT) is a special type of therapy developed specifically for people with BPD. DBT focuses on acceptance of the condition and its effects, followed by developing ways to solve problems and change behavior. It combines individual therapy with group treatment to help patients learn skills to help them cope better with their condition. Early studies of DBT suggest that it may be an effective treatment for this mental health disorder.

According to the NIH, the outlook for curing BPD is poor. Because of the nature of the disorder, many BPD patients do not comply with their doctors' orders.

Other Types of Personality Disorders

In addition to BPD, there are many other types of personality disorders. A few of these types of disorders are described here.

Antisocial Personality Disorder

Antisocial personality disorder is a condition in which people manipulate, exploit, or violate others. Many people with this disorder repeatedly break the law. They are unconcerned about their own safety and the safety of those around them. They do not feel guilty about or ashamed of their behavior.

Whether it's tagging a wall with graffiti (which a worker cleans here) or committing far more serious offenses, people with antisocial personality disorder tend to have little regard for the law or for the property of others.

Researchers believe that abuse or neglect suffered as a child may contribute to the development of antisocial personality disorder later in life. Symptoms of the condition usually peak in a person's late teens or early twenties. The condition affects men more often than women. According to the NIH, it is a common condition among people in prison.

Experts consider antisocial personality disorder to be the most difficult type of personality disorder to treat. Most people who suffer from the disorder do not seek treatment on their own. In many cases, those who do receive treatment are ordered to do so by a court of law. People with the condition often have substance abuse problems and legal problems that result from their disorder.

Paranoid Personality Disorder

People with *paranoid* (PAAR-uh-noyd) *personality disorder* are overly suspicious and untrusting of others. In addition, they may have low self-esteem, feel detached from those around them, and be hostile to others. People suffering from paranoid personality disorder have difficulty in work and social situations and may not seek medical attention because of a distrust of doctors.

Schizoid Personality Disorder

People with *schizoid* (SKIT-zoyd) *personality disorder* are indifferent to other people, even family members, and often isolate themselves. Some researchers believe that this disorder is in some way tied to schizophrenia. People with this disorder rarely seek treatment.

Dissociative Disorders

Dissociative (diss-OH-see-uh-tiv) *disorders* are mental health disorders that disrupt a person's sense of identity or self. People with a dissociative disorder lose touch with who they are and who they once were. They may separate events that happened to them from their own lives.

Many people have experienced mild dissociation. When people become so lost in thought that everything around them fades or they no longer feel like themselves, they are experiencing dissociation. Severe dissociative disorders, however, cause serious disability. They can disrupt a person's family, work, and social relationships.

Certain groups of people are at a higher risk for dissociative disorders. Those who have suffered from physical or sexual abuse during childhood or who have suffered a severe trauma are more likely to develop these mental illnesses. Some researchers believe that a dissociative disorder may be the brain's way of protecting an individual from these terrifying incidents. Types of dissociative disorders include dissociative identity disorder, dissociative amnesia, dissociative fugue, and depersonalization disorder.

Dissociative Identity Disorder

According to the National Association for the Mentally Ill (NAMI), *dissociative identity disorder* (DID) is a disturbance of identity in which two or more separate and distinct personality states control an individual's behavior at different times. A person with DID may have as few as two or as many as 100 separate identities or personalities. DID was previously called *multiple personality disorder.*

Women are much more likely to develop DID than men are. In fact, some sources say that nine out of ten patients with this disorder are female. DID is usually the result of chronic childhood abuse, often by loved ones. The condition usually develops during childhood but is often not diagnosed until much later.

Each of the patient's personalities has its own separate history and characteristics. For example, an alternate personality might know only parts of a patient's past. Each alternate personality usually has a different name and may speak differently, exhibit different behaviors and habits, and even be a different gender.

One symptom of DID is periods of amnesia. A patient with DID may lose track of periods of time when another personality is in control. In fact, a person with this disorder might seek professional help for these gaps in time without being aware of the condition. As a result of the time loss, people with DID might meet other people who claim to know them, find themselves somewhere without knowing how they got there, or find items that they don't remember purchasing. Patients with DID are often affected by other mental health conditions, as well, including mood, anxiety, and conduct disorders.

DID can be treated. The most common treatment is long-term, frequent psychotherapy with a mental health professional. Hypnosis may also be a part of the treatment. When treating DID, the goal of the therapist is to merge the many personalities into one. This process is known as *integrating*.

Dissociative Amnesia

Dissociative amnesia (am-NEE-zhuh) is memory loss caused by a traumatic event. The person suffering from the condition is often unable to remember important information that is related to the trauma in some way.

There are a number of different types of dissociative amnesia.

- *Generalized amnesia*—A person cannot recall his or her entire life.
- *Localized amnesia*—A person cannot recall a traumatic event.
- *Selective amnesia*—A person cannot recall certain parts of a traumatic event.
- *Systematized amnesia*—A person cannot recall information about a specific object, place, or person.

Many cases of dissociative amnesia are short-lived, lasting for twenty-four hours or less. Some cases, however, last for years. When dissociative amnesia persists, the patient should be treated by a mental health professional. Doctors treat the condition with therapy and sometimes with hypnosis.

Dissociative Fugue

Dissociative fugue (fyoog) is a disorder in which a patient loses his or her identity, leaves home, and travels to a new location. The journey from one place to another can last for hours, days, or even months. In rare cases, the patient assumes a new identity.

A traumatic or stressful event often triggers a dissociative fugue. Once the fugue state is over, people may not remember where they traveled or what they did during the journey.

Depersonalization Disorder

A *depersonalization* (dee-per-sun-ul-ih-ZAY-shun) *disorder* is a disorder in which people feel detached from their bodies and selves. The feelings recur over and over, causing patients to feel as if they are stuck in a dream or "going crazy." The length of an episode can vary from a few minutes to a few days. The feelings gradually disappear, only to recur later. For some people, the episodes become so severe that they lead to disability and loss of function.

Depersonalization may be triggered by a traumatic event, such as a natural disaster or a violent crime. Treating the condition can be difficult. Therapy to learn coping strategies can be helpful to patients. In some cases, doctors prescribe antianxiety drugs.

CHAPTER 4
Anxiety Disorders

An *anxiety* (ang-ZYE-ih-tee) *disorder* is a mental health condition that causes a person to feel extremely anxious or fearful. Anxiety disorders are among the most common of mental health disorders: each year, about 19 million Americans are affected by some type of anxiety disorder.

Anxiety disorders can interfere with a person's ability to lead a normal, healthy life. These conditions can cause uncomfortable physical and emotional symptoms. There are several different types of anxiety disorders, including generalized anxiety disorder, panic disorders, obsessive-compulsive disorder, post-traumatic stress disorder, and phobias.

Generalized Anxiety Disorder

Generalized anxiety disorder (GAD) is a mental health condition in which a person constantly feels anxious. Worried thoughts persist day after day and interfere with the patient's normal routine. A person with GAD worries about even the smallest, most inconsequential things that could go wrong. In some cases, the patient worries about just getting through the day.

In addition to worried thoughts, anxiety, and tension, people with GAD may experience physical symptoms, such as sweating, shaking, feelings of fatigue or nausea, headaches, and muscle pains. GAD may also affect a person's ability to relax, concentrate, or sleep.

GAD is a fairly common mental health disorder. As many as 4 million adult Americans suffer from the condition. Twice as many women suffer from GAD as men. Although the disorder can occur at any age, most people develop GAD between childhood and middle age.

Many people with GAD realize that their worrying is out of control. They know that the worrying is making their lives more difficult. However, they are unable to put a stop to the tension and anxiety by themselves.

Doctors diagnose GAD after a patient has spent at least six months worrying about common, everyday events. Because GAD often occurs with other mental health disorders, especially other anxiety disorders, doctors will look for those, as well. A physical test to rule out other medical conditions is usually performed.

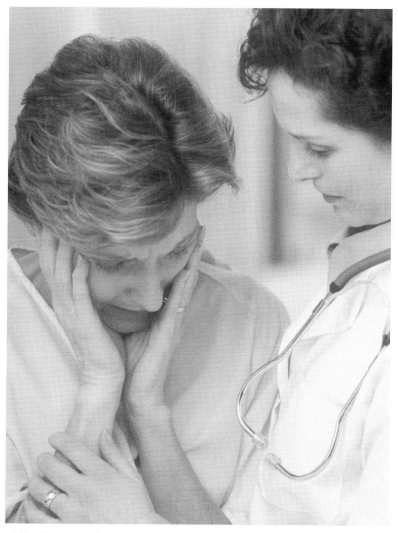

Although many people whose lives are affected by constant anxiety know that their anxiety is out of control, they may find it almost impossible to stop worrying. A diagnosis of generalized anxiety disorder can start a patient on the road to relief from symptoms.

For most patients, medication brings relief from the symptoms of this disorder. The most common types of drugs prescribed for GAD sufferers include antidepressants and antianxiety drugs. In addition, doctors may recommend special types of relaxation therapy, including meditation and deep-breathing exercises.

Panic Disorder

Panic disorder is a type of anxiety disorder that involves sudden, severe episodes of fear and dread. These episodes are sometimes called *panic attacks*. The attacks can last for a few minutes or several hours. Most attacks peak within ten minutes.

Researchers are not sure what causes panic disorder, but there seems to be a genetic factor involved. Environment and learning also seem to play a part in this disorder. Doctors do know that women are twice as likely to suffer from panic disorder as men are.

Most people first develop panic disorder before the age of twenty-five. Children can also be affected by this mental health condition. Symptoms of a panic attack include shortness of breath, dizziness, rapid heartbeat, trembling, chills or sweating, feelings of choking, nausea, and chest pains. During panic attacks, people may feel as if they are dying, losing control, or going crazy.

The symptoms of panic disorder can be so devastating that people may develop anxiety about having another attack. They may therefore avoid going to school, work, or social events. When a person becomes unwilling to venture outside for fear of having a panic attack, the condition is known as agoraphobia. About one-third of all patients with panic disorders develop agoraphobia.

Like some other mental health disorders, panic disorders can lead to substance abuse. People may begin abusing alcohol and other drugs to try to numb the feelings of fear. Substance abuse can lead to other mental and physical problems.

Diagnosing and Treating Panic Disorder

To diagnose a panic disorder, doctors will first perform a thorough physical examination in order to rule out all other disorders and illnesses. Once the doctor has determined that a person is suffering from a panic disorder, treatment can begin. In many cases, antianxiety and antidepressant medications will help. Therapy may also be recommended. During therapy, patients learn relaxation techniques and other methods that they can use to lessen anxiety.

Research has shown that people can ease the severity of a panic disorder by taking good care of their bodies. Exercise, a healthful diet, and plenty of sleep can all help. Doctors also recommend that people with panic disorder avoid foods with caffeine.

Fast Fact

About 2 percent of the U.S. population experiences a panic disorder in any given year.

Obsessive-Compulsive Disorder

Obsessive-compulsive (ubb-SESS-iv kum-PUL-siv) *disorder* (OCD) is a type of anxiety disorder in which a person is unable to control certain thoughts, images, or behaviors. Uncontrollable thoughts that constantly invade the consciousness (KAHN-shuss-ness) and cannot be ignored are called *obsessions.* Uncontrollable behaviors—such as counting something over and over—are called *compulsions* (kum-PUL-shunz). Although people with OCD may recognize that their thoughts or actions are irrational or unhealthy, they cannot do anything to stop them.

More than 3 million adult Americans suffer from OCD. The disorder usually develops between the ages of twenty and thirty. However, children can also suffer from OCD. Researchers do not know what causes OCD. There may be a genetic factor, because the disorder seems to run in some families.

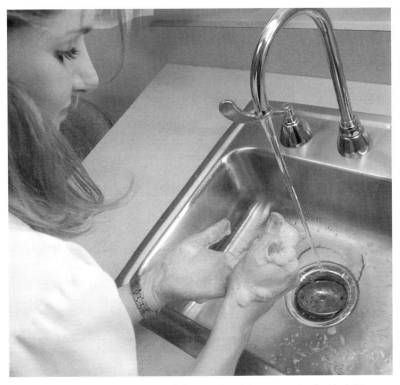

Repeated hand washing is typical of the compulsive behaviors associated with OCD, which, along with obsessive thoughts, make life difficult for people with the disorder. Though sufferers know their behavior is unhealthy, they cannot control it.

OCD affects a person's ability to lead a healthy, normal life. A person whose thoughts and actions begin interfering with day-to-day functioning needs to seek professional help. To diagnose OCD, doctors must first rule out other health conditions by performing physical and other exams.

Patients with OCD are usually treated with a combination of antidepressant drugs and therapy. During therapy, OCD sufferers learn better, less harmful ways to reduce their feelings of anxiety and fear. Although the condition is treatable, it is difficult to cure. OCD sufferers may also have other mental health disorders, including depression, other anxiety disorders, substance abuse disorders, and eating disorders.

Are You Overstressed?

Stress is a normal part of most people's daily lives. Events like preparing for a big test or auditioning for the school play can cause a person to become worried and anxious. In some situations, stress is positive. It may motivate some people to try harder and do their best.

Stress becomes a problem when it causes mental or physical health problems. How can you tell if there's too much stress in your life?

- You find yourself losing your temper more easily than normal—even over small things.
- You begin getting headaches or an upset stomach.
- You feel sad or anxious much of the time.
- You have difficulty paying attention and may begin to forget things.
- You have problems getting to sleep at night or have frequent nightmares.

Post-Traumatic Stress Disorder

Post-traumatic stress disorder (PTSD) is an anxiety disorder that develops after an especially terrifying or traumatic event. People with PTSD relive the event through troubling thoughts, memories, dreams, or *flashbacks*. Flashbacks are episodes in which people feel that they are once again experiencing the event. Events that can trigger PTSD include violent crimes, disasters, accidents, and military combat.

Symptoms of PTSD may occur soon after the event or may develop months later. Most people begin experiencing symptoms within three months of the traumatic event. PTSD symptoms fall into one of three general categories.

- *Repeated reliving of the event*—Thoughts, memories, dreams, and flashbacks are all ways that PTSD patients relive an event. People may also experience physical reactions to events that bring back memories of the trauma.

- *Avoidance*—Fearfulness, depression, hopelessness, and the deadening of normal emotions fall into the avoidance category. Patients may also stay away from people, places, or objects that remind them of the trauma that they have suffered.

- *Arousal*—People may have difficulty sleeping, overreact to things that startle them, and have sudden outbursts of temper. In addition, patients may become excessively vigilant in an attempt to avoid future trauma.

Other symptoms include guilt and such physical conditions as headaches, heart palpitations, dizziness, fainting, paleness, and fever. PTSD symptoms may become more severe around the anniversary of the traumatic event.

Feelings of distress, sadness, and anger after a disaster or other terrifying event are normal. Having these feelings does not mean that a person has PTSD. When the feelings persist and affect a person's ability to function, however, it is time to talk to a friend or family member or consult a mental health professional.

Survivor's Guilt

After living through an accident, a disaster, or some other life-threatening event, some people are affected by an emotion that is sometimes called "survivor's guilt." People with survivor's guilt wonder why they were spared from harm while others suffered. Rescue workers and those who have had a loved one die may also suffer from survivor's guilt.

Survivor's guilt is a normal part of grieving. People can work through this emotion by talking to others about their feelings. If the feelings of guilt and sadness persist, people should talk to a mental health professional.

Who Is at Risk for PTSD?

Each year, more than 5 million American adults develop PTSD. People of all ages, races, and social status can develop the condition. However, women are twice as likely to suffer from PTSD as men.

Not everyone who witnesses a traumatic event will develop PTSD. Genetic, psychological, physical, and social factors all seem to play a role in determining who develops the condition. Recent research has revealed that adults who suffered from abuse as children are more likely to develop PTSD. Other studies are looking to connect the development of PTSD with abnormal brain functioning or unusual hormone levels in some people.

Some jobs put people at an increased risk of developing PTSD. For example, military personnel, firefighters, police officers, and rescue workers are routinely exposed to terrifying, traumatic events. Research suggests that as many as one out of every three rescue workers suffers from some of the symptoms of PTSD.

Victims of sexual assault and other violent crimes are also at high risk for PTSD. It is essential for those who have been victimized to talk to others about their feelings and to seek professional help if necessary.

Studies have shown that strong social support helps protect some people from this condition. Those who talk about the trauma with friends and family soon after it occurs are thought to fare better than those who don't. For this reason, many communities offer counseling or crisis intervention after disasters.

Fast Fact

One million U.S. military veterans developed PTSD after serving in Vietnam during the Vietnam War (1964–1975).

PTSD and the Civil War

From 1861 to 1865, the United States was ripped apart by a war that pitted the North against the South. Thousands of Americans lost their lives during the war, and thousands more returned home carrying scars that would last a lifetime. What doctors of the time didn't know was that many Civil War veterans had suffered much more than physical wounds during the bloody conflict.

In the nineteenth century, doctors knew little about how trauma can affect a person's mind and health. They had no knowledge of the damage that can be caused by warfare and violence. In recent years, however, historians have looked back to determine whether Civil War veterans might have suffered from what we now call PTSD.

Historian Eric Dean pored over Civil War medical reports and memoirs to find hints of mental illness, particularly PTSD. Because doctors didn't have modern terms to label mental

It is likely that PTSD has always affected soldiers returning from war.
Here, the granddaughter of a Vietnam veteran visits the Vietnam Veterans Memorial
in Washington, D.C. The names of veterans who died as a result of PTSD and
other ailments were recently added to the list of Americans who died in the war.

problems, Dean found conditions described as insanity, soldier's heart, melancholy, homesickness, dementia, and sunstroke. Other soldiers, possibly mentally unwell, were labeled "cowards" or "malingerers."

Dean also explored the medical records of 291 Union soldiers confined to the Indiana Hospital for the Insane. He determined that many of them displayed symptoms that today would probably lead to a diagnosis of PTSD.

Diagnosing and Treating PTSD

Before diagnosing PTSD, doctors usually perform physical and psychiatric examinations to rule out other medical conditions. Doctors diagnose PTSD if the patient has a history of having suffered a serious trauma recently, accompanied by symptoms of the disorder.

Mental health professionals treat PTSD with therapy. They encourage patients to talk about the trauma, to express their feelings, and to learn to gain control over the event. This type of therapy is called cognitive-behavioral therapy. Antidepressant and antianxiety medications are also used to ease PTSD symptoms.

Some people with PTSD recover without any help. More often, some therapy or other assistance is needed. The earlier PTSD is diagnosed and treated, the greater the chances of recovering from the condition.

Patients with PTSD may develop other mental health conditions, including depression, other anxiety disorders, and substance abuse disorders. These other disorders need to be diagnosed and treated, as well.

Children and PTSD

In addition to disasters, exposure to extended violence or abuse at home, at school, and in the community can cause children serious distress and, in some cases, lead to PTSD. Even seeing graphic news reports of disasters on TV or in the newspaper can cause some children to develop the condition.

For children, early treatment is especially important in easing the distressing symptoms of PTSD. The NIMH has the following tips for adults who want to help children heal after violence, disaster, or another traumatic event.

- Explain the violence or disaster as well as you are able.
- Encourage children to express their feelings. Listen to them without passing judgment. However, do not force them to talk about the event.
- Let children know that it is normal to feel upset after a traumatic event.
- Reassure them that the disaster is not their fault.
- Allow children to cry and be sad. Don't expect them to be brave or tough.

Recent studies have shown that with the proper help and support, most children and adolescents recover from a disaster within a few weeks and do not develop the symptoms of PTSD. Even with support, however, some children still develop the condition.

Fast Fact

Inner-city children are exposed to more violent acts than children living in other areas of the United States. One recent study reported that 68 percent of young adolescent boys in Chicago, Illinois, had witnessed someone being beaten up. More than 20 percent had seen someone shot or killed.

9/11 and PTSD

On September 11, 2001, terrorist attacks on the World Trade Center in New York City left approximately 2,800 people dead. People around the nation and the world grieved for those who lost their lives in the disaster.

The disaster also affected the mental health of many people—particularly New Yorkers. Weeks after the attacks, researchers found that the rates of depression and PTSD for people living near the World Trade Center were twice as high as the national average. The rate of cigarette, alcohol, and drug use also increased dramatically.

In 2003, the pain still lingered for many New Yorkers. Research showed that of all people who developed PTSD after September 11, those who lost a loved one, lost a job, or experienced stress after the attacks were most likely to still be suffering from symptoms of PTSD. Studies also suggested that people under the age of thirty and over the age of sixty were likely to still be experiencing symptoms of PTSD.

Phobias

Phobias (FOH-bee-uhz) are extreme, unreasonable reactions to objects or situations that pose little or no danger. When people with phobias come in contact with the things that they are afraid of, they may experience severe anxiety or even suffer a panic attack. To avoid these feelings, people with phobias may do their best to avoid places and situations that might bring them into contact with the things that they fear. This can seriously interfere with a person's life.

Phobias are some of the most common mental health disorders. As many as 10 percent of the U.S. population are affected by such a condition. Phobias are especially common in children. However, most children eventually outgrow these mental health conditions.

Although many cases of phobia are chronic, people with this condition can be treated successfully. One treatment for phobias is known as systematic desensitization (dee-sen-sih-tih-ZAY-shun). With this treatment, patients are taught to relax and then gradually confront the things that frighten them. Over time and with practice, the fear should lessen.

*In a form of graded real-life exposure, a woman participates
in a class for people with aquatic (water) phobias.*

Another method for treating phobias is known as *graded
real-life exposure*. With this method, people are gradually
exposed to the things that frighten them. For example, a person
who is afraid of snakes might first be shown photos of snakes.
Later, the person might visit a zoo with a therapist and watch
live snakes in captivity. If the treatment is very successful, the
patient might eventually be able to see a snake without feeling
overwhelmed by fear and anxiety.

In recent years, researchers have been examining the
possibility of using virtual reality to treat phobias. Virtual reality
uses computer images to graphically simulate real experiences.
In one early study, people with a fear of heights were helped by
putting on headsets that made them feel as if they were on
bridges, elevators, or balconies—but all in a safe, computerized
environment. Virtual reality also seemed to reduce people's
agoraphobia and fear of flying. Researchers are currently testing
whether other phobias can be lessened with this technology.

In severe cases of phobias, where the patients' lives are being affected, doctors might prescribe antianxiety or antidepressant medication. These drugs relieve the symptoms of phobias. People with the most severe phobias are less likely to be treated successfully.

There are three basic types of phobias: social phobia, agoraphobia, and specific phobias.

Social Phobia

Social phobia is a common anxiety disorder. People with social phobia fear being embarrassed in public. As many as 13 percent of all American adults will experience this condition at some point in their lives.

Social phobia is more serious than shyness. Social phobia can cause such physical symptoms as heart palpitations, blushing, sweating, diarrhea, and muscle tension. It can even lead to a panic attack. To avoid these uncomfortable symptoms, people with social phobia try to stay away from situations in which they have to appear in front of others. They may avoid public speaking, parties, dining in public, or meeting new people. The condition may also lead to substance abuse because adults with social phobia may use alcohol or other drugs to loosen up in social situations.

Adults and adolescents with social phobia may be able to control their fear. Children, however, usually cannot. Their symptoms may include crying, clinging, tantrums, and avoidance. These can cause problems at school and with social interactions.

Doctors believe that many cases of social phobia begin during adolescence. The condition may be caused by overprotective parents or by not having enough opportunities to participate in social situations.

Agoraphobia

Agoraphobia (agg-uh-ruh-FOH-bee-uh) is a fear of being in a place where help or escape, if necessary, is not available. Such places include crowded buildings, bridges, buses, and other public areas.

Agoraphobia usually occurs with another anxiety disorder, particularly panic disorder or another phobia. The condition affects women more often than men. Because some people with agoraphobia refuse to leave their homes, the disorder can seriously disrupt their lives.

Physical symptoms of agoraphobia include sweating, dizziness, nausea and vomiting, a rapid pulse, high blood pressure, and chest pains. Emotional symptoms of the disorder include feelings of helplessness, a feeling that the body or the surrounding environment is unreal, feelings of detachment from others, and dependence upon others.

Specific Phobias

People can develop fears of nearly anything in their environment. The fear of an object or situation is known as a *specific phobia,* or a *simple phobia.* As with other phobias, people with specific phobias realize that their fears are irrational. However, they are unable to control their feelings of terror.

Symptoms of specific phobia include anxiety, sweating, rapid heartbeat, avoidance of feared situations, and poor motor control when exposed to the feared object. Although phobias are often chronic, they can be treated so that the patient's school, work, and social interactions are not seriously affected.

Some Specific Phobias

Here are a few common specific phobias:
- Acrophobia (ak-roh-FOH-bee-uh)—fear of heights
- Claustrophobia (kloss-truh-FOH-bee-uh)—fear of being in an enclosed or small space
- Pterygophobia (tayr-ih-goh-FOH-bee-uh)—fear of flying
- Ophidiophobia (oh-fid-ee-oh-FOH-bee-uh)—fear of snakes

- Arachnophobia (uh–rak–noh–FOH–bee–uh)—fear of spiders
- Cynophobia (sin–oh–FOH–bee–uh)—fear of dogs
- Zoophobia (zoh–oh–FOH–bee–uh)—fear of all animals

Separation Anxiety

Separation anxiety is a fear of being separated from a primary caregiver, such as a parent or other relative. Children between the ages of eight months and two years commonly develop separation anxiety. At this age, the condition is considered a normal part of development. Toddlers with separation anxiety are usually fearful of new situations and new people.

Most children outgrow separation anxiety without treatment. In older children, the condition may recur when they are feeling stressed or unsafe, especially when a parent is not present. When the condition persists and the child is older than two years of age, parents may wish to talk to their doctor or another medical professional.

Symptoms of separation anxiety include nightmares, extreme upset when separated from the caregiver, constant worrying about the caregiver, reluctance to go to school or other places, reluctance to sleep alone at night, and physical ailments.

To treat separation anxiety, doctors usually recommend counseling for the child and family. In serious cases, they may prescribe antianxiety medications and suggest more intensive therapy.

CHAPTER 5
Cognitive Disorders

Cognitive (KOG-nih-tiv) *disorders* are conditions that affect a person's ability to think, speak, and remember. They can also affect a person's judgment, self-control, and social functioning. These disorders include amnesia, delirium, dementia, and Alzheimer's disease.

Amnesia

Amnesia is a loss of short- and long-term memory. People with this condition are unable to learn new information or recall information that they once knew. Amnesia is often caused by brain trauma or another underlying medical condition. However, amnesia can also be caused by a severe emotional trauma.

Some medical conditions that cause amnesia are Alzheimer's disease, head injury, seizures, alcohol and drug abuse, stroke, and brain infections. Aging can also cause amnesia.

Doctors often talk about two different types of amnesia, anterograde and retrograde. *Anterograde amnesia* is the inability to remember ongoing events that occur *after* a specific injury or illness. *Retrograde amnesia* is the inability to remember events that occurred *before* a specific injury or illness. Depending upon the cause, amnesia can affect a person suddenly or develop slowly. The underlying cause also affects whether the amnesia is temporary or permanent. To treat amnesia, doctors diagnose and treat the underlying cause of the condition.

Delirium

Delirium (deh-LEER-ee-um) is a short-lived condition that is marked by rapidly shifting mental states. The condition usually appears suddenly. Symptoms of delirium include disorganized thinking, inability to concentrate, disorientation, hallucinations, changed sleeping patterns, loss of short-term memory, changes

A young woman suffering from amnesia returns to her home in Florida after being found in a hospital in New York City more than a month after she disappeared.

in movement, and personality changes. Those most at risk for delirium are men and women over the age of sixty.

Delirium is most often the result of another physical or mental health condition. The most common medical causes of delirium include fever, lack of oxygen, and brain infections. The condition may also be caused by a variety of other factors, including alcohol and drug use or injury. Delirium can worsen if the patient is in an unfamiliar and frightening setting, such as a hospital.

Doctors treat delirium by identifying and treating the underlying problem that has caused the condition. During treatment, the patient's environment should be made as comfortable and nonthreatening as possible. Sedatives and other medications may be used to calm the patient. The condition usually lasts for about a week, but it may take much longer for the patient to recover from the episode.

Dementia

Dementia (deh-MEN-shuh) is a group of symptoms that involves the impairment of a person's brain functions. Emotions, as well as the ability to speak, think, and remember, can all be affected. Dementia is often caused by another medical condition. It can also be caused by alcohol or drug abuse. Whether dementia can be successfully treated depends upon the underlying problem that is causing the dementia. In fact, the leading cause of dementia is Alzheimer's disease, which is not curable.

Although dementia is not a normal result of aging, the condition usually worsens as time goes on. The elderly are at especially high risk. Up to 8 percent of people over the age of sixty-five have some form of dementia.

The first symptoms of the condition are usually forgetfulness, insomnia, and irritability. People may then lose problem-solving abilities, followed by the deterioration of language skills. Eventually, the condition affects people's daily activities, making it difficult for them to function normally. Other symptoms include loss of memory, inability to concentrate, confusion, hallucinations, delusions, impaired motor skills, and changes in personality.

Doctors diagnose dementia in a person when at least two different brain functions are affected. While there is usually no cure for the condition, doctors will try to control dementia and prevent it from becoming worse. Medications to control unsafe behaviors and calm the patient may be prescribed if necessary. Therapy is usually not effective.

Alzheimer's Disease

One of the most serious cognative disorders is *Alzheimer's* (AHLZ-hye-merz) *disease*. Alzheimer's is a progressive brain disorder that currently affects as many as 4 million Americans. The disease most often progresses slowly, robbing patients of their memories and seriously impairing such brain functions as

A man in the first stages of Alzheimer's disease listens with his wife to a speaker at the New Mexico state capitol on Alzheimer's Day, organized to raise awareness of the disease.

thinking, speaking, concentrating, and making decisions. People with Alzheimer's may also suffer personality changes.

Alzheimer's is a physical condition that causes both structural and chemical problems in the brain. The disease destroys *neurons* (NOOR-onz), or nerve cells, in the brain. This loss, in turn, leads to a decreased production of *neurotransmitters* (noor-oh-TRANZ-mit-erz), the chemical messengers that carry impulses from one neuron to another.

No one knows what causes Alzheimer's disease. Risk factors include old age and a family history of dementia. The older a person gets, the more likely that he or she will develop Alzheimer's disease. Nearly half of all people over the age of eighty-five have Alzheimer's. Because women live longer than men, they are more likely to be affected by the condition. However, doctors stress that Alzheimer's is not a normal part of the aging process.

Fast Fact

According to the Alzheimer's Organization, about 14 million Americans will have Alzheimer's by the year 2050 unless a cure or method of prevention is found.

Types and Stages of Alzheimer's Disease

Doctors recognize two different types of Alzheimer's disease: early-onset and late-onset. Patients with *early-onset* Alzheimer's usually develop the condition before the age of sixty. This type of Alzheimer's seems to run in some families, so it may be genetic. Early-onset Alzheimer's is less common than late-onset: only about 5 to 10 percent of all Alzheimer's patients have this form of the disease.

Patients with *late-onset* Alzheimer's usually develop the condition after the age of sixty. Late-onset Alzheimer's is less likely to run in families, and genetics play less of a role. Late-onset Alzheimer's is much more common than early-onset.

The progression from the earliest stages of Alzheimer's to the latest stages can take up to twenty years. However, most people with Alzheimer's live about eight years after developing the condition. Doctors at the New York University Medical Center's Aging and Dementia Research Center have developed a scale to help health care professionals accurately assess a patient's condition. The scale, called the Functional Assessment Staging (FAST) scale, categorizes the progression of Alzheimer's into sixteen different stages.

The FAST Scale

FAST Stage	Characteristics
1 Normal adult	No decline in function
2 Normal adult	Personal awareness of functional decline

3 Early Alzheimer's	Deficits noticed in demanding work situations
4 Mild Alzheimer's	Requires assistance with complicated tasks
5 Moderate Alzheimer's	Requires assistance choosing proper attire
6 Moderately severe Alzheimer's	
6a	Requires assistance dressing
6b	Requires assistance bathing properly
6c	Requires assistance with mechanics of using the toilet
6d	Urinary incontinence
6e	Fecal incontinence
7 Severe Alzheimer's	
7a	Speech ability limited to about a half-dozen intelligible words
7b	Intelligible vocabulary limited to a single word
7c	Ambulatory ability lost
7d	Ability to sit up lost
7e	Ability to smile lost
7f	Ability to hold up head lost

The Ten Warning Signs of Alzheimer's

As people get older, it is normal for them to have some changes in memory. Alzheimer's disease, however, is not a normal part of aging. The Alzheimer's Organization has developed a list of ten warning signs that a person may have Alzheimer's.

1. Memory loss—Patients forget recently learned information and do not remember it later.

2. Difficulty performing familiar tasks—Patients forget how to do such everyday tasks as preparing a meal or taking part in a lifetime hobby, things that they once did without thinking.

3. Problems with language—Patients forget simple words or substitute unusual words. As a result, their speech and writing become difficult to understand.

4. Disorientation in time and place—Patients become lost on their own street. They forget where they are, how they got there, and how to find their way home.

5. Poor or decreased judgment—Patients may begin dressing inappropriately for the weather or giving away large amounts of money to telemarketers and salespeople.

6. Problems with abstract thinking—Such tasks as balancing a checkbook become nearly impossible because patients do not know what the numbers are or what to do with them.

7. Misplacing things—Patients begin to put things in unusual places. They may, for example, put an iron in the refrigerator.

8. Changes in mood or behavior—Patients begin suffering rapid mood swings for no apparent reason.

9. Changes in personality—Patients may grow more difficult and demanding, often becoming suspicious, confused, or fearful.

10. Loss of initiative—Patients become unwilling to do even the least demanding of activities, choosing instead to sit in front of the TV or sleep all the time.

Diagnosing and Treating Alzheimer's

There is no positive test for Alzheimer's. Doctors make the diagnosis based on the patient showing symptoms of dementia, accompanied by memory loss. After death, a sample of the patient's brain tissue can be examined to confirm the Alzheimer's diagnosis.

A researcher at the University of Kentucky performs a test. In this lab, scientists discovered a protein that may be related to the onset of Alzheimer's disease, thus taking one small step toward the prevention of the disease. There is currently no cure.

Early diagnosis of Alzheimer's is important. The earlier the patient is diagnosed, the sooner that treatment and control of the symptoms can begin. Doctors usually diagnose the condition after determining that the patient is suffering from dementia. Then health professionals will work to find out what exactly is causing the dementia. They will perform physical and mental examinations of the patient to exclude other possible causes of the dementia.

There is currently no way to prevent or cure Alzheimer's disease, and lost abilities can never be restored. The goal of treatment is to slow the course of the disease and control its progress. To do this, doctors will prescribe one of three medications currently approved for use with the disease. In addition, health professionals can work with patients to help them with behavior problems and managing confusion.

When a person has Alzheimer's, life can be very difficult for those around him or her. At some point, the family will probably be unable to care for the Alzheimer's patient at home. Watching the effects of this debilitating condition on a loved one, as well as the decision to send a loved one to a nursing or convalescent home, can cause depression, anxiety, and other problems.

Health professionals recommend that friends and family members of Alzheimer's patients seek support for themselves. Support groups, counseling, or conversations with a trusted friend can ease the sadness and frustration that are common for Alzheimer's caregivers. Learning as much as possible about Alzheimer's can also help people prepare for what is to come during the course of the illness.

CHAPTER 6
Attention Deficit Hyperactivity Disorder and Learning Disabilities

Some of the most common conditions to affect school-aged children are ADHD and learning disabilities. Learning disabilities affect the way that a person interprets and connects information. About 4 million American children suffer from learning disabilities. These disorders can persist into adulthood and continue to cause problems.

Attention Deficit Hyperactivity Disorder

Attention deficit hyperactivity disorder (ADHD) is the most commonly diagnosed mental health problem in American children. According to the NIMH, as many as 5 percent of all school-aged children in the United States suffer from this disorder. Past research has indicated that ADHD affects boys three times as often as it affects girls. More recent research, however, indicates that boys and girls may be equally affected by the disorder.

ADHD affects a person's ability to remain focused on a single task. It also affects a child's ability to control impulses and maintain a normal level of activity. As a result, patients with ADHD are unable to concentrate for extended periods. They may be hyperactive, easily distracted, or impulsive.

Children with ADHD often do poorly in school. They may be unable to sit still and pay attention to lessons. Students with ADHD are often punished for this behavior, even though they cannot help it. Children with ADHD may have problems in other areas of life, as well. They may have difficulty forming relationships with other children. Their disorder may also cause conflict and problems at home.

As children with ADHD become older, problems caused by the disorder do not disappear. Adolescents with ADHD are at

A seven-year-old with ADHD talks to his mother. Like many other kids with ADHD, he dislikes school and says his favorite part of the day is after school, when he can play. ADHD makes it hard for children to sit still and focus, so they find school difficult.

higher risk for motor vehicle accidents, tobacco use, and early pregnancy. ADHD can also continue into adulthood. In fact, more than half of all children with ADHD will continue to suffer from the condition as adults. According to a group called Children and Adults with Attention Deficit Hyperactivity Disorder (CHADD), between 2 and 4 percent of American adults are affected by ADHD.

What Causes ADHD?

Researchers are not sure what exactly causes ADHD. Because the disorder tends to run in families, many believe that there is a genetic factor. Children who have ADHD usually have at least one close relative who also has the condition.

Researchers have also noticed that the brains of children with ADHD are about 5 percent smaller than the brains of other children. In addition, the part of the brain that controls concentration and attention is less active in ADHD children.

In the past, many people were quick to blame ADHD on an unstable or dysfunctional home life, but recent research has found that this is not the cause. Research has also shown that watching too much TV or eating a diet that is high in sugar does not cause ADHD. However, some symptoms associated with ADHD can be caused by diet—too much sugar or certain food colorings can cause temporary symptoms.

Diagnosing and Treating ADHD

To diagnose ADHD, doctors look for one or more of the following three major symptoms.

- *Inattention*—People with ADHD have a hard time focusing on a single task for very long. They become bored easily and have difficulty completing lessons, chores, and jobs. Learning new things can be a problem.
- *Impulsivity*—People with ADHD have difficulty controlling their reactions to people and events around them. Schoolchildren may be restless while waiting on line or blurt out answers in class.
- *Hyperactivity*—People with ADHD feel the need to be constantly active and always on the move. They have a hard time sitting still for very long: they may squirm, tap their toes, jiggle their legs, or show other signs of being uncomfortable. Hyperactivity often decreases with age.

Not everyone who is inattentive, hyperactive, or impulsive has ADHD. Anxiety, stress, depression, boredom, or another learning disability can also cause these symptoms. A physical condition, such as an ear infection or a seizure disorder, may also be to blame. It's important for doctors to eliminate other causes before diagnosing ADHD.

To determine whether or not a person has ADHD, doctors need to know how long the symptoms have existed, how severe these symptoms are, and whether the symptoms occur in many different settings. To get this information, doctors will talk to the patient, parents, and teachers in order to learn the patient's history.

Many children with ADHD have or develop other mental health conditions, such as oppositional defiant disorder (ODD), anxiety disorders, and depression. Doctors usually watch for signs of these other problems.

It is important that a child with ADHD be diagnosed and treated. The most common treatment for ADHD is drugs. In most cases, the drugs reduce hyperactivity and help ADHD sufferers concentrate. These drugs should be taken only while a patient is under a doctor's care. Doctors may also recommend psychotherapy to complement the medicine.

Is It "Just a Phase"?

Doctors usually do not diagnose preschool children with ADHD. The normal behavior of a preschool child may mimic the condition. Also, other problems at this age (language delays, developmental delays) can have the same symptoms. Some teens also go through developmental phases that mimic the symptoms of ADHD. For this reason, doctors must carefully test children and teens before diagnosing them with ADHD.

ADHD in the News

Over the last decade, ADHD has received much attention. Increased information about the disorder has led to more children being diagnosed with ADHD. Doctors are not sure whether the number of children with the disorder is rising or whether diagnoses are just becoming more accurate.

Some people believe that many doctors are incorrectly diagnosing ADHD in children who actually suffer from other problems. These people feel that a quick diagnosis of ADHD with a prescription for unnecessary medication is the wrong way to fix unacceptable behavior at school or home.

Ritalin, one of the drugs used to treat ADHD, has come under fire. When used for long periods of time, Ritalin can have serious side effects, including high blood pressure, increased heart rate, tremors, mood changes, personality changes, and severe weight loss. In addition, Ritalin can be abused, and some people become addicted to it. Some people believe that Ritalin and other drugs should not be prescribed for children.

To better understand ADHD and find more effective ways to treat this disorder, researchers continue to seek more information about what causes the condition. Studies on the effects of toxins, alcohol, and other drugs on fetuses may help researchers to better treat those suffering from ADHD in the future.

Learning Disabilities

A *learning disability* is a disorder that affects a person's ability to interpret information properly, or learn. Although most children with these disorders have normal intelligence, learning disabilities keep them from being academically successful. For children suffering from learning disabilities, school becomes frustrating, and self-esteem plummets. They may develop emotional problems as a result of learning disabilities.

The federal government defines a learning disability as a significant gap between a child's intelligence and the skills that he or she has achieved at a given age that is not caused by another condition. If a second grader has average intelligence, for example, yet fails to master the math skills that other average second graders have mastered, the child may have a type of learning disability.

A failure to achieve at the expected level becomes a serious problem when it persists and leads to academic failure and social difficulties for a child. In the early elementary grades, a two-year difference between the child's achievement and normal achievement is a warning sign of a learning disability.

Learning disabilities have many different symptoms. Children with learning disabilities may be unable to understand and follow directions. Letters, numbers, and other symbols may not make sense to them. They may seem withdrawn, quiet, or in a world of their own—or they may be overactive, unable to sit still, or always in trouble. There are usually no physical symptoms to indicate that a child has a learning disability.

There are different types of learning disabilities. The three major categories are developmental speech and language disorders, academic skills disorders, and any other disorders not covered by the first two categories.

Developmental Speech and Language Disorders

Developmental speech and language disorders are learning disabilities that affect a person's ability to speak and understand spoken language. With *developmental articulation disorder,* children have problems controlling their rate of speech. They may not develop speech as quickly as others their age, or they may have problems with certain sounds. For example, a child with a developmental articulation disorder may say "weady" instead of "ready." This type of disorder affects about 10 percent of all children younger than eight years of age. Most children outgrow this disorder or can be helped with speech therapy.

Children with *developmental expressive language disorder* have problems expressing themselves with spoken words. A child with this type of disorder might call something by a wrong name, speak only in short sentences, or be unable to respond to simple questions.

Children with *developmental receptive language disorder* may have difficulty understanding spoken words. This is not because the child has a hearing problem. Instead, the child cannot make sense of the sounds or words.

Academic Skills Disorders

Academic skills disorders are disorders that impair a child's ability to learn. They can affect a child's reading, writing, or mathematical abilities. Some children may have problems in more than one area.

Also called *dyslexia* (diss-LEKS-ee-uh), *developmental reading disorder* is a common learning disability that affects between 2 and 8 percent of all elementary school children. The disorder is a result of a child's brain not being able to properly process letters and other symbols. The disorder can affect a child's word identification and comprehension.

Developmental writing disorder affects a child's ability to write words. The child often cannot compose a complete, grammatically correct sentence. *Developmental arithmetic disorder* affects a child's ability to recognize numbers, memorize facts, or grasp mathematical concepts.

Other Learning Disabilities

Other types of learning disabilities can also affect children. For example, some children have disorders that affect their motor or coordination skills. Children with these disorders may lack

Kids with learning disabilities of all kinds can participate and do well in school activities. Since the young boy's learning disabilities include physical challenges, his physical therapist sits next to him.

coordination, have problems with their penmanship, or have difficulties with spelling and memorization.

What Causes Learning Disabilities?

Doctors are not sure what causes children to develop learning disabilities. Some researchers believe that the disorders are caused by problems with the way that the brain develops or functions. These problems probably occur when the child is still inside the mother's womb.

Because learning disabilities tend to run in some families, researchers believe that the disorders may have a genetic component. Research is also being conducted to see if learning disabilities are caused by a mother's use of alcohol or other drugs during pregnancy. Problems during a child's birth or toxins that are present in the child's early environment may also play a part. Researchers are currently examining whether exposure to cadmium and lead could cause such disabilities.

Diagnosing and Treating Learning Disabilities

Learning disabilities can be treated successfully. It is important for parents and teachers to understand that with the proper help, children with learning disabilities can learn. With treatment, these children can learn how to be successful in school.

Without treatment, learning disabilities can continue to affect children after they have grown into adolescence and adulthood. An adult with a learning disability may experience problems communicating with others, learning new tasks, or completing known tasks at work.

Learning specialists diagnose learning disabilities using standardized tests. The results of the tests are compared to average results for children of the same age. Next, the specialists determine which type of learning disability a child has. Determining this may require visits to a speech therapist for speech testing, a psychologist for intelligence testing, and a physician to make sure that there aren't any physical conditions causing the problems.

Treatment of a learning disability depends upon the severity of the problem, as well as the wishes of the child's family. At school, a special education program can help students find ways to strengthen their skills and learn successfully. Some families hire a tutor to help their children after school. There are also schools that specialize in teaching children with learning disabilities. Over time, learning disabled students can learn how to cope with the disorder by focusing on the positives and developing the skills that they do have in order to strengthen those that are weak.

Safeguarding the Rights of the Learning Disabled

The United States has a number of laws that protect the rights of people with learning and other disabilities. In the early 1990s, Congress passed laws that protect children with learning and other disabilities. The Individuals with Disabilities Education Act of 1990 requires public schools to provide learning disabled students with educational programs that fit their individual needs. A year later, another act made these programs available to children as young as five years old.

Other legislation protects learning disabled people on the job and at college. One act prevents employers from discriminating against learning and other disabled people. Other laws require colleges to admit and work with learning disabled students. Some colleges now have special programs designed specifically for learning disabled students.

CHAPTER 7

Pervasive Development Disorders and Mental Retardation

Pervasive development disorders (PDDs) are brain disorders that affect as many as 6 children out of every 1,000. PDDs are sometimes known as *autistic* (aw–TISS–tik) *spectrum disorders.* These disorders most often affect a child's communication and social skills. Symptoms of a PDD usually are first noticeable when a child is about three years old. Perhaps the most well-known type of PDD is autism. Other types include Asperger's syndrome, Rett syndrome, and childhood disintegrative disorder.

Autism

Autism (AW–tiz–um) is a brain disorder that affects the normal development of social and communication skills. Autism is a physical condition caused by problems in the brain's structure or functioning. As many as two out of every 1,000 Americans have autism, and boys are more likely to have the disorder than girls are.

Researchers don't know what causes autism. There may be a strong genetic factor to the condition: autistic children often have relatives with language and learning disorders, as well as some other disorders. In addition, families with one autistic child are more likely to have a second autistic child. Some researchers think that autism might also be caused by medical problems or conditions that the child's mother develops during her pregnancy. Such problems include the disease rubella or lack of oxygen to the baby during labor and delivery. Researchers continue to search for answers regarding the causes of autism.

Cases of autism can range from very mild to severe. People with mild autism are able to speak and have normal or high intelligence. As adults, they can usually lead independent, fulfilling lives. People with more severe forms of autism are sometimes said to be "low functioning." They may also suffer from mental retardation, seizure disorders, and other medical conditions.

The first signs of autism usually appear before children are three years old. Some parents begin to worry that there is a problem when their child is still an infant. In other cases, children seem fine until they are one or two, and then suddenly begin displaying symptoms of autism. This type of autism is known as *regressive autism*.

Certain behaviors—impaired social interactions, impaired communication skills, and restricted and repetitive behavior—are common to all people who have autism. Other symptoms include aggressive behavior, a lack of interest in imaginary play or imitating others, heightened or decreased senses, a withdrawal from physical contact, and tantrums.

Diagnosing and Treating Autism

Doctors become concerned when children fail to reach certain developmental milestones (such as babbling or gesturing) or regress to an earlier stage of development. Before diagnosing

Developmental delays are one of the first signs for doctors that a child may have autism. Here, a mother works with her six-year-old autistic son as she writes words and he spells along with her. He cannot write the letters, but is practicing saying them.

autism, however, doctors will first perform physical, developmental, and neurological (noor-oh-LAH-jik-ul) tests on children to rule out other medical conditions. These tests include blood tests, hearing tests, and a screening test for autism. Neurological tests check brain and nervous system function.

There is currently no known prevention or cure for autism. When treating this condition, the goal is to help autistic people function at their highest levels. The earlier treatment begins, the better the chances of success. Special education programs, along with behavioral therapy, have been shown to help. Various medications are also available to treat the condition. Most people with autism are able to remain with their families or live independently.

Asperger's Syndrome

Asperger's syndrome is a PDD in which children have difficulty knowing how to behave socially. Some researchers believe that the condition is a mild form of autism. More boys than girls are affected by this disorder.

Symptoms of Asperger's syndrome include impaired nonverbal communication skills, such as the ability to make eye contact; limited use of facial expressions; clumsy or awkward movements; a failure to develop relationships with other children; an inability to reciprocate social or emotional feelings; repetitive behaviors, including snapping or twisting the fingers; and a preoccupation with one specific subject or area of interest.

Children with Asperger's have the ability to learn and care for themselves. With training and assistance, most can learn to control the symptoms of the condition and live an independent and fulfilling life. However, children with Asperger's are at an increased risk of developing other mental health conditions later in life.

Rett Syndrome

Rett syndrome is a PDD that affects only girls. Rett syndrome results in mental retardation and regression from earlier levels of development.

During the first few months of life, the infant develops normally and there are no signs that anything is wrong. Symptoms of Rett syndrome usually arise between six and eighteen months of age. One of the first warning signs of the disorder is *hypotonia* (hye-poh-TONE-ee-uh), or decreased muscle tone. Infants with this condition have floppy limbs and poor head control.

Other symptoms of Rett syndrome include slowed head growth around the age of six months, regression to earlier stages of physical and emotional development, loss of language skills, loss of meaningful use of the hands, breathing problems, and—in one out of three patients—seizures. Although Rett syndrome usually stops progressing when a girl reaches adolescence, the condition always results in severe mental retardation. Most children become completely unable to care for themselves.

The condition is biological, caused by the mutation of a single gene. (A *mutation* is a change in a gene that leads to new traits in offspring. Radiation, chemicals, environmental factors, and accidents to unborn young can all cause mutations.) The abnormal gene causes brain damage as the child matures. Most of the mutations are spontaneous, which means that they are not caused by an inherited condition.

There is currently no cure for Rett syndrome. Doctors treat the condition with different types of physical and behavioral therapy to help affected children function at their highest potential. There are also medications that can be prescribed to help prevent seizures and breathing problems.

Childhood Disintegrative Disorder

Childhood disintegrative disorder (CDD) is a PDD that begins to affect children at the age of three or four years old. It results in a permanent loss of physical, social, language, and other abilities.

Like children with Rett syndrome, children with CDD develop normally during the first months of life. They usually stop developing between the ages of eighteen and thirty-six months. Symptoms of CDD include loss of motor skills, bladder control, language skills, self-care skills, and social skills. Other symptoms include failure to play and develop relationships with peers.

No one knows what causes CDD. Researchers believe that the disorder may be related to neurological problems. Although CDD is rare, some cases may be misdiagnosed as autism because the symptoms are so similar.

Mental Retardation

Mental retardation is a developmental disorder in which a person tests well below average on mental ability or intelligence tests and has impaired ability in communication, self-care, or social and school settings. Mental retardation is most often diagnosed in infancy or childhood, but always occurs before age eighteen. As many as 3 percent of all Americans are affected by mental retardation.

Cases of mental retardation can range from mild to severe. Children with mild cases are likely to have a lack of curiosity and be very quiet. Children with severe cases display infantlike behavior throughout their lives. Severe cases are usually detected earlier than milder cases. Most parents or caregivers begin to notice that there is something wrong when their children fail to reach normal developmental milestones at the same time as most other children. Mild cases, however, may not be recognized until children begin school.

The cause of about 75 percent of all cases of mental retardation is unknown. Risk factors for this condition include injuries that occur before, during, or after birth; infections; brain abnormalities; and exposure to toxins. Some of the most common known causes of mental retardation are Down's syndrome, fragile X syndrome, and fetal alcohol syndrome. Boys are more likely to be affected by mental retardation than girls are.

While most cases of mental retardation cannot be prevented, others can. For example, mental retardation caused

Many mentally retarded people function well and enjoy the same activities as others without disabilities. This Ohio teen participated in his first football game and was allowed to score a touchdown for his team.

by fetal alcohol syndrome could be avoided if pregnant mothers stopped drinking alcohol. Medical conditions in infants that can lead to mental retardation should be treated soon after birth.

Doctors diagnose mental retardation by performing developmental and intelligence tests. Because people with mental retardation may also have other medical conditions, such as cerebral palsy, seizure disorders, vision and hearing impairment, or ADHD, doctors will test for these, as well. People with severe cases of mental retardation are more likely to have one or more of these other medical conditions.

Once doctors have diagnosed mental retardation, children can begin receiving training and special education to help them develop to their fullest potential. As adults, many people with mental retardation can live independent, fulfilling lives. Others, however, may need to live in a supervised environment for the rest of their lives.

CHAPTER 8
Eating Disorders

An *eating disorder* is a mental health condition in which patients practice seriously unhealthy eating habits that they can no longer control. Some people severely limit the amount of food that they eat. This can lead to undernourishment and other nutritional deficiencies. Other people overeat, causing obesity and other health conditions. (Obesity is the condition of being excessively overweight.) Eating disorders often occur with other mental health problems, such as depression, substance abuse, and anxiety disorders.

In the United States, eating disorders are becoming more common. According to the National Association of Anorexia Nervosa and Associated Disorders (ANAD), about 6 million Americans suffer from eating disorders. Eating disorders usually first appear in adolescence. The disorders usually affect young women, but they can affect men, as well. The three most common types of eating disorders are anorexia nervosa, bulimia nervosa, and binge eating disorder.

Fast Fact

Fourteen- and fifteen-year-old girls are more likely to develop eating disorders than any other group.

Anorexia Nervosa

Anorexia nervosa (an-uh-REKS-ee-uh ner-VOH-suh) is a disease in which people starve themselves in order to become thin. Even when patients become dangerously underweight, they continue to believe that they are too fat. An estimated 90 to 95 percent of anorexia sufferers are female.

People with anorexia develop an obsession with eating and food. Other symptoms of the disease include refusal to gain weight, constant fear of being fat, irregular menstrual periods, and excessive exercise. Later symptoms include dizziness, fainting, memory loss, confusion, and inability to concentrate.

Anorexia is a serious health condition. A person who doesn't eat properly is not getting enough of the important nutrients needed to allow the body to function correctly. Improper eating habits can lead to such serious health complications as malnutrition, dehydration, kidney failure, heart problems, and osteoporosis. *Osteoporosis* (ah-stee-oh-puh-ROH-siss) is a musculoskeletal (mus-kyoo-loh-SKEL-uh-tul) condition in which the bones become thin and fragile. The most severe cases of anorexia lead to death. Studies suggest that 5 percent of all people suffering from anorexia die as a result of the condition.

Symptoms of an Eating Disorder

Warning signs of an eating disorder include the following:

- Extreme and dramatic weight loss
- Constant expressions of feeling fat, denying hunger, or anxiety about weight gain
- Preoccupation with food, calories, and nutrition
- Irregular or absent menstrual periods
- Wanting to eat alone or eating secretly
- Compulsive eating, whether hungry or not
- Binge eating followed by purging
- Depression or anxiety
- Brittle hair or nails; loss of hair
- Frequent use of the bathroom after eating
- Signs of frequent vomiting, including reddened fingers or puffy cheeks

Bulimia Nervosa

Bulimia nervosa (bul-EE-mee-uh ner-VOH-suh) is a disease in which a person binges upon food and then either purges the food from the body, fasts, or strenuously exercises. Purging is vomiting or using medications such as laxatives or diuretics to rid the body of food. *Fasting* is not eating for a period of time. Like those suffering from anorexia, bulimics are obsessively concerned with the shape and size of their bodies. As with anorexia, most patients suffering from the condition are young women. ANAD estimates that 5 percent of all female college students suffer from this condition.

Symptoms of bulimia include puffy cheeks or glands caused by frequent vomiting, stained or discolored teeth, and withdrawal or depression. Like anorexia, bulimia can lead to serious health problems, including heart disorders, esophageal inflammation, digestive disorders, blood pressure abnormalities, and erosion of tooth enamel. It can also lead to heart failure and death.

Binge Eating Disorder

Binge (binj) *eating disorder* is a condition in which people have frequent episodes of uncontrolled, or binge, eating. During these eating binges, they will eat more than is necessary to satisfy their hunger. After each binge, patients may feel guilty and unhappy.

Binge eating is one of the most recent eating disorders to come to the attention of health professionals. Although the condition is not accepted as a medical problem by all doctors, the National Institute for Diabetes and Digestive and Kidney Diseases (NIDDK) believes that binge eating affects as many as 4 million people in the United States—2 percent of all Americans. Binge eating, which is also a feature of bulimia nervosa, affects men and women, although some studies suggest that 60 percent of all sufferers are female. Binge eating is the most common eating disorder.

Binge eating disorder, a component of bulimia nervosa, is often characterized by secretive eating. Many people who suffer from this kind of eating disorder realize that they have a problem and work to conceal it from others.

Most of the people who suffer from this condition are overweight or obese. Doctors are not sure what causes people to become binge eaters, but depression may be a factor. Symptoms of the disorder include eating large amounts of food at one sitting, eating more quickly than normal, eating alone, and feelings of guilt and depression after bingeing.

Like other eating disorders, binge eating can have serious health consequences. It can lead to high blood pressure, high cholesterol levels, heart problems, diabetes, and gallbladder disease. As with all eating disorders, people who have binge eating disorder should see a doctor for treatment of the physical and psychological aspects of the condition.

Helping Someone with an Eating Disorder

If you believe that a friend has an eating disorder, here are some tips on how to help from the National Eating Disorders Association (NEDA).

- Set aside some private time to talk with your friend about your worries.

- Explain that you are concerned about your friend's well-being. Cite specific examples from the past that you think might indicate an eating disorder. Explain that the friend's problem can be helped with professional treatment.

- Ask your friend to explore these concerns with someone who knows more about eating disorders. Counselors, doctors, dieticians, and other health professionals can help. Eating disorders can pose serious health risks. If you are concerned about a friend—or even yourself—make sure to get help from one of these adults.

Treating Eating Disorders

Eating disorders are treatable. However, treatment for anorexia, bulimia, and binge eating disorder can often prove difficult because patients may not believe that there is anything wrong with them. As a result, they may resist treatment that could help them recover. Doctors say the earlier that patients are diagnosed and begin treatment, the greater the chances of a successful recovery.

For anorexia and bulimia, hospitalization may be an important part of the healing process, especially if the patient is malnourished and needs immediate medical attention. Once a person's physical state has been stabilized, counseling is another important part of the treatment. Working with mental health professionals, patients are taught healthier eating habits and learn how to accept their bodies as they are. The ultimate goal of counseling is to eliminate unhealthy eating habits and unrealistic images of the body. In some cases, medications may speed up the healing process.

CHAPTER 9
Disruptive Disorders

Disruptive disorders are mental health conditions in which a person displays aggressive or antisocial behavior. These types of disorders often develop at an early age. Disruptive disorders include oppositional defiant disorder and conduct disorder.

Oppositional Defiant Disorder

Oppositional defiant disorder (ODD) is a disruptive disorder that causes a child to consistently act out or misbehave. A child with ODD may overreact and become physical when upset or angry. Other symptoms of the disorder include irritability, stubbornness, defiance, and hostility.

In very young children, oppositional or defiant behavior is normal. A toddler who is refused a cookie, for example, may have a temper tantrum. If the child's tantrums are ignored but do not subside over a reasonable period of time, the child may have a more serious problem. If the child's behavior is frequent, continues for more than six months, and begins to affect family, school, or social life, help is needed.

Before puberty, ODD most commonly affects boys. Most boys with ODD develop the disorder by age eight. After puberty, boys and girls are equally affected by the disorder. A child or adolescent with ODD is more likely to develop a conduct disorder later in life.

Researchers are not sure what causes ODD. There is some evidence, however, that a child whose parents have marital problems, who has had many different caregivers, or who has experienced inconsistent or unsupervised child rearing is at a higher risk for the condition. Biological factors may also play a role.

```
╭─────────────────────────────────────────────╮
              Fast Fact
╰─────────────────────────────────────────────╯
```

Nearly half of all children with ADHD also have ODD. Children
with these two disorders are at a higher risk for getting in serious
trouble at school and in other settings.

Conduct Disorder

Conduct disorder is a type of disruptive disorder in which
children violate the rights of others, disregard rules, and break
laws. They may get into fights or bully other students at school.
They may vandalize property or set fires. They may skip school,
shoplift, use alcohol and illegal drugs, or engage in early sexual
activity. These harmful activities interfere with children's ability
to succeed in school, at home, and in the community at large.

According to the surgeon general's report on mental health,
between 1 and 4 percent of nine- to seventeen-year-olds have a
conduct disorder. The same report states that this mental health
condition is more common in urban areas than rural areas. Boys
are more likely to develop conduct disorder than girls are. In
addition, children who develop this disorder early in life are
more likely to develop antisocial personality traits as adults.

Girls with conduct disorder may run away from home and
become involved in prostitution. Both girls and boys with
conduct disorder are at an increased risk of depression and
suicide attempts. They also have higher injury rates and are
more likely to be expelled from school, engage in criminal
behavior, or contract a sexually transmitted disease.

Although it is not known for sure what causes conduct
disorders, researchers believe that biological and psychosocial
(sye-koh-SOH-shul) factors both play a part. Biological risk
factors include ADHD, learning problems, insensitivity to
physical pain, or brain damage caused by low birth weight or
problems during birth. Psychosocial factors include maternal
rejection; separation from parents with no alternative caregiver;
family neglect, abuse, or violence; large family size; poverty; or

parental marital problems. These problems can lead children to feel unattached to their parents or family and eventually to disregard rules and laws.

Children aged eleven to thirteen with conduct disorders often exhibit aggressive behavior when they are much

A child with an untreated conduct disorder is likely to grow into a teen, and later an adult, with antisocial personality traits. These often include a willingness to engage in criminal behavior.

younger—even as young as three years old. If mental health workers can diagnose a conduct disorder early, the chances of working with parents and patients to successfully treat the condition improve. Children suffering from these disorders can be helped socially and academically from an early age to increase their chances for success.

The Effects of Bullying

One common symptom of a conduct disorder is aggression toward animals or other people. One type of aggressive behavior is bullying. Many U.S. children say that bullying is one of the biggest problems that they have to deal with at school each day.

This high school student said she was often the victim of bullying in middle school. She managed to end her torment and gain confidence by standing up for herself and not letting a bully's problem become her own.

Bullying is any act of physical, verbal, or emotional violence that is intended to hurt someone. Pinching, shoving, hair-pulling, and name-calling are all bullying. Leaving people out of group activities or spreading gossip about them is bullying behavior, too. Although boys are more likely to be involved in bullying behavior, girls can also be bullies and victims of bullying, as well.

Bullying is serious. It can lead to self-esteem problems by robbing the bullied person of self-respect. A bullied person can suffer from nightmares, illness, and poor grades. Bullying can also lead to violence, physical injury, and even death. Recent studies have shown that bullies and their victims are at a higher risk of taking part in violent activities later in life, including fighting and carrying weapons.

Experts on childhood violence say that all threats of violence made by bullies need to be taken seriously. This means reporting the threats to a teacher, guidance counselor, or another adult who can take action.

Treating Disruptive Disorders

ODD and conduct disorders are most often treated with training and therapy. The most effective treatments for disruptive disorders are parent training programs. In these programs, parents learn to deal with their children more effectively. They are taught to reward positive behaviors and ignore or punish negative behaviors. Parent training also serves to strengthen the bond between parents and child. For the patient, anger management training and other behavioral therapy may be helpful.

In recent years, researchers have studied the effects of certain medications on children with disruptive disorders. So far, none have been found to consistently decrease aggressive behavior.

Do Boot Camps Work?

In some parts of the nation, adolescents with conduct disorders are sent to military-style behavior camps, also known as wilderness therapy or, more commonly, boot camp. At boot camps, children must follow a rigid schedule and take part in strenuous exercises meant to instill discipline, self-esteem, and an appreciation of life back home. If the children get out of line, they are subjected to harsh punishments. Children sent to these camps usually spend between four weeks and six months there.

To some parents, boot camp seems like a good way to help difficult children. However, the camps can be dangerous and even deadly. A number of children in the United States have died as a result of conditions at boot camps that they attended. Further, research has failed to prove that boot camps improve the behavior of children with conduct disorders. In fact, recent research suggests that children with such conditions who attended boot camps later had lower rates of employment and higher rates of felony arrest.

CHAPTER 10
Substance Abuse Disorders

A *substance abuse disorder* is a mental health condition in which a person becomes psychologically (sye-koh-LAH-jik-lee) dependent upon alcohol or other drugs. People with such a mental health condition crave the drug, feeling that they must have it in order to feel good. The drug use begins to negatively affect the person's relationships and activities.

Some people with drug abuse disorders also become physically dependent upon the drug. This happens when the body begins to build up a tolerance to the drug. As a result, users need more and more of the drug to make them feel good. When people with a physical dependence on a drug try to stop using it, they suffer from withdrawal symptoms. *Withdrawal* is a state of physical and mental distress. Symptoms of withdrawal include shaking, sweating, and diarrhea.

A substance abuse disorder can affect every aspect of a person's life. It interferes with relationships and leads to problems at work, at school, at home, and in the community. For people with substance abuse disorders, the most important thing in their lives is obtaining and using their drug of choice. They may begin to steal or lie to get the money that they need to buy drugs.

Stages of Drug Abuse

According to the NIH, there are several stages leading from drug use to drug abuse. Research has shown that juveniles progress more rapidly through the stages than adults.

- *Experimental use*—Drug use at this stage is recreational and usually involves peers. Juveniles may be using the drugs to defy a parent or other authority figure.

- *Regular use*—Juveniles use drugs to ease negative feelings. They begin skipping school or work and isolating themselves from friends and family. Instead, they may begin to hang out with peers who also use drugs regularly.

- *Daily preoccupation*—At this stage, juveniles become obsessed with using drugs. They lose all interest in friends, school, work, and activities that they once enjoyed. In order to earn money to buy drugs, they may sell drugs to others. They may also begin using more dangerous drugs.

- *Dependence*—At this stage, juveniles believe that they cannot make it through the day without drugs. Their physical and mental health continues to deteriorate. They may become suicidal and have numerous legal and financial problems.

Who Is at Risk for a Substance Abuse Disorder?

Doctors are not sure why some people develop substance abuse disorders while other people who use drugs do not. Many researchers believe that some people have a genetic predisposition to become addicted to drugs. Other risk factors for substance abuse include low self-esteem, poverty, friends or family members who use drugs, and family instability or divorce.

Some drugs are naturally more addictive than others. Crack cocaine and heroin, for example, can lead to dependency much more quickly than other types of drugs. Unfortunately, many people—especially teens—believe that they can handle their drug use and that addiction is something that will not happen to them.

The use of so-called gateway drugs also puts people—especially teens—at risk for substance abuse disorders. Studies have shown that gateway drugs, which include cigarettes, alcohol, and marijuana, can lead people to try more dangerous drugs, such as cocaine or heroin.

Law-enforcement and other officials speak about the growing problem
of cocaine and heroin abuse in their state. The chart shows the dramatic
increase in deaths caused by cocaine in Florida over a seven-year period.

Recognizing a Substance Abuse Disorder

Do you think someone that you care about might have a substance abuse disorder? The following are some of the warning signs for this condition.

• Withdrawal from relationships with friends and family

• A loss of interest in things that were once enjoyable

• Anxiety or depression

• Poor academic performance

• Secretive behavior

• Friends who also use drugs

• Mood swings

• A change in sleeping or eating habits

Substance Abuse and Other Mental Health Conditions

One risk factor for substance abuse problems is another mental health disorder. The existence of two mental health disorders at one time, such as substance abuse and major depression, is called a *dual diagnosis*. A recent study revealed that between 41 and 65 percent of all adults suffering from substance abuse disorders also had a lifetime history of at least one other mental health issue. The same study found that about half of all people who have a mental health disorder will have at least one substance abuse disorder at some point in their lives. One theory accounting for this correlation (kor-uh-LAY-shun) between substance abuse and other mental health problems is that patients with mental health disorders may use alcohol and other drugs in order to "self-medicate," or make themselves feel better.

Children and teens are also affected by substance abuse and mental health disorders at the same time. Studies have indicated that half of all young people diagnosed with a substance abuse disorder were also suffering from another mental health condition. These conditions included depression and other mood disorders; anxiety disorders; and ADHD.

Drug Abuse Statistics

- One out of four high school seniors has used illegal drugs.
- In 1999, there were 175,000 cocaine-related emergency room visits in the United States.
- The same year, there were more than 19,100 drug-induced deaths across the nation.
- The use of marijuana, alcohol, and cigarettes by the nation's eighth, tenth, and twelfth graders declined from 2001 to 2002.

Treating Substance Abuse Disorders

There is hope for people with substance abuse disorders. In recent years, health professionals have gained new insight into which treatments work best. The goal of any type of substance abuse treatment is to treat both the physical and mental aspects of the disease. Treatment is aimed at helping patients conquer drug cravings and preventing a relapse of drug use.

Most substance abuse disorder patients are treated with a combination of behavioral therapy and medications. Behavioral therapies include psychotherapy, individual counseling, group or family counseling, and support groups. Researchers have found that one of the most effective therapies for teens and adolescents with substance abuse disorders is family-oriented therapy. With this type of therapy, both the patient and the patient's family receive counseling.

Medications are effective with substance abuse patients who are addicted to certain types of drugs. People addicted to heroin, for example, are often treated with a drug called *methadone* (METH-uh-dohn). Methadone is a synthetic opiate that suppresses cravings and other withdrawal symptoms associated with heroin addiction.

There are a number of different ways that substance abuse patients can receive their treatment. *Residential therapy* is a method in which the patient is confined to a hospital or clinic during part of the treatment. These stays generally last six months or less. Another type of treatment is drug-free outpatient treatment. With this method, the patient visits a counselor or therapist periodically for psychotherapy but does not need medication.

Substance abuse treatment can be a long, difficult process. A number of treatments may be necessary. For those people who suffer from a substance abuse disorder along with another mental health condition, treatment is especially important. Health professionals agree that the conditions should be treated at the same time.

CHAPTER 11
Schizophrenia

Schizophrenia (skit-zuh-FREE-nee-uh) is a group of brain disorders that affect a person's thoughts, behaviors, and personality. People with schizophrenia have difficulty telling the difference between real experiences and the hallucinations that are often part of the disorder. Schizophrenia can affect every aspect of a person's existence. It impairs one's ability to maintain normal relationships, to think logically, and to function properly in social situations.

Schizophrenia often prevents its victims from leading a normal life. The delusions and hallucinations associated with it leave a person disoriented and unable to function properly. While there is no cure, there are treatments that can control these symptoms.

Experts do not know what causes schizophrenia. Because schizophrenia tends to run in some families, researchers believe that some people may be genetically predisposed to the disease. Other researchers believe that environmental factors, such as fetal infection or problems during the birth process, may play a part. Recent research has shown that the disorder may be caused by an abnormality of the brain that occurs during fetal development.

Schizophrenia is one of the most severe and disabling forms of mental illness. One out of every 100 Americans suffers from schizophrenia, and some studies suggest that about 1 percent of the world population may be affected by the disease, as well. It is one of the top ten causes of disability worldwide.

Most people develop schizophrenia before the age of forty-five. The condition often begins during adolescence and peaks between the ages of fifteen and thirty. Men and women are equally at risk of developing the condition. Women, however, tend to develop schizophrenia later than men.

Facts about Schizophrenia

- Schizophrenia does not mean that a person has a split personality.
- Most people with schizophrenia are not a danger to others.
- Taking drugs does not cause schizophrenia, but it can worsen the condition.
- The actions of parents, relatives, or friends do not cause schizophrenia.

Symptoms of Schizophrenia

Schizophrenia usually develops slowly, with symptoms becoming more serious over a period of months or years. Because the symptoms worsen gradually, many people do not notice the early symptoms of the disease.

- *Delusions*—The patient has false beliefs or thoughts that have no basis in fact.
- *Hallucinations*—The person hears, sees, or feels things that are not there.
- *Disordered thinking*—The person may be unable to concentrate on one subject for long and may be easily distracted. Thoughts jump from one topic to another that is completely unrelated. As a result, speech may not seem to make sense.
- *Disorganized or erratic behavior*—The patient may move more slowly than other people or may repeat certain movements, such as pacing or walking in circles.
- *Negative, or flat, affect*—The person displays no emotions and seems to lack expression. He or she may show a lack of interest in the surrounding world.

People with schizophrenia are at an increased risk of suicide. In fact, 10 percent of all people diagnosed with the disease commit suicide—especially young adult males. Some people with schizophrenia also suffer from substance abuse disorders. The use of alcohol and other substances can make the symptoms of schizophrenia worse. Some substances interfere with the effectiveness of medications used to treat the condition. Substance abuse also lessens the chance of the patient continuing with the treatment.

Many people with schizophrenia also are addicted to nicotine. The rate of tobacco use among schizophrenics is three times higher than that of the rest of the U.S. population. Like other substances, cigarettes can interfere with the effectiveness of medications used to treat the condition. Studies have shown that patients who smoke need higher doses of medicine.

Types of Schizophrenia

Doctors recognize five different types of schizophrenia.

- *Catatonic* (kat-uh-TAHN-ik) *schizophrenia*—Symptoms include motor disturbances, stupor, negativism, rigidity, excitement, inability to take care of personal needs, restlessness, and decreased sensitivity to pain.

- *Paranoid schizophrenia*—Symptoms include delusional (deh-LOO-zhun-ul) thoughts of persecution or grandeur, anxiety, anger, violence, and arguing.

- *Disorganized schizophrenia*—Symptoms include incoherence, regressive behavior, flat affect, delusions, hallucinations, inappropriate laughter, repeated rhythmic gestures and behaviors, and social withdrawal.

- *Undifferentiated schizophrenia*—The patient may display symptoms of several different types of schizophrenia.

- *Residual schizophrenia*—Prominent symptoms from a previous diagnosis are mostly eased, but some features remain.

Schizophrenia in Children and Adolescents

Childhood onset schizophrenia is a rare type of the disease that affects children between the ages of seven and twelve. Children with schizophrenia suffer serious problems in their day-to-day existence. Symptoms include hallucinations, delusions, flat affect, and social withdrawal. Like adults with the disorder, schizophrenic children are at a higher risk for suicide.

Because the disease so rarely affects children, childhood onset schizophrenia may be initially mistaken for another disorder, such as autism. This type of schizophrenia is more difficult to treat than other types. However, treatment options have improved in recent years. Researchers are currently testing whether new medications are effective in treating this serious disease.

In adolescents, schizophrenia is often overlooked at first. Early symptoms of schizophrenia, such as subtle personality changes, may be attributed to the process of growing up. Indeed, these changes may be noticed only after they persist and begin to affect a teen's life.

Diagnosing and Treating Schizophrenia

Before making a diagnosis of schizophrenia, doctors will perform physical and psychiatric tests to rule out other medical conditions. Doctors may also decide to order *computerized tomography* (tuh-MAH-gruh-fee), or CT, scans of the patient's head. These imaging tests allow them to see if the patient's brain shows any of the physical changes that are associated with schizophrenia.

Once these tests have been done, doctors will check if the patient's problems meet the criteria for schizophrenia. These include having two or more of the symptoms of schizophrenia for one month or longer and a loss of ability to function in social and work settings. If a patient has been having delusions or auditory hallucinations in which two voices talk to each other or one voice talks to the patient, doctors can immediately make a diagnosis of schizophrenia.

There is currently no cure for schizophrenia. Doctors can, however, treat the disease and make life more bearable for those who suffer from it. The goal of treatment is to control the symptoms and improve the patient's ability to think clearly.

The usual treatment for people suffering from schizophrenia is a combination of medications and therapy. Drugs used to treat the condition work by changing the balance of chemicals in the brain. Many of these drugs have serious side effects, however, so some schizophrenic people choose not to take them. Researchers are currently testing new drugs that may be more effective in treating teens with schizophrenia.

Therapy can benefit schizophrenics (skit-zuh-FREH-niks) by providing support and helping them take control of some parts

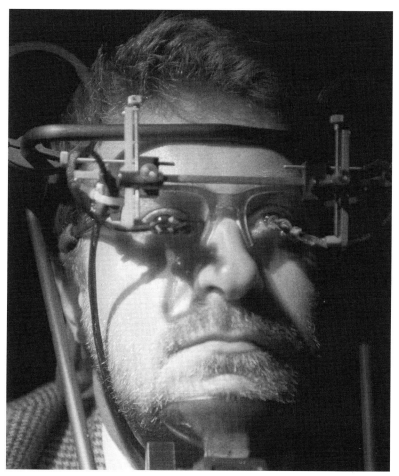

A doctor in New York demonstrates a device that shows how well a person's eyes track a moving laser dot. This test may help identify those who are at a high risk for developing schizophrenia.

of their lives. In addition, research has shown that people who have a strong support network of friends and family members are less likely to have severe schizophrenic symptoms recur.

People who are suffering from severe symptoms of schizophrenia need to be hospitalized to keep them from harming themselves and others. In the hospital, patients can be cared for properly. Patients with the most severe cases of schizophrenia may need to live in group homes or other supervised homes where they can receive treatment and care.

Schizoaffective Disorder

Schizoaffective (skit-zoh-uh-FEK-tiv) *disorder* is a mental health condition in which a patient displays symptoms of schizophrenia along with some symptoms of an affective mood disorder, such as major depression or bipolar disorder. Like schizophrenia, schizoaffective disorder is a serious condition that can cause people to lose the ability to function well. The disorder is rare in children.

Symptoms include depression, angry outbursts, mania, delusions, and hallucinations. With medication and therapy, patients with schizoaffective disorder can be treated successfully. However, treatment may need to continue for the rest of a patient's life.

Brief Psychotic Disorder

Brief psychotic disorder is a condition in which a patient suddenly displays psychotic symptoms. The symptoms last for at least several hours, but no longer than one week. The patient usually develops the condition after a traumatic event, such as a disaster or the death of a loved one. During a psychotic episode, patients may or may not know that they are behaving strangely.

People are more likely to experience brief psychotic disorder in adolescence or early adulthood. People with personality disorders are at a higher risk for developing the condition.

Doctors diagnose brief psychotic disorder after ruling out other conditions and determining whether or not patients have a history of recent stress in their lives. Although symptoms usually subside with time, doctors may treat the patient with medications to ease any current symptoms. Therapy can also help the patient learn to handle stress. Without therapy, the person may experience future episodes in response to stressful events.

CHAPTER 12
Impulse-Control Disorders

An *impulse-control disorder* is a mental health condition in which people give in to impulses that they know are harmful. There are several different types of impulse-control disorders.

Compulsive Gambling

Compulsive gambling is a condition in which a person cannot resist the urge to gamble. Unlike casual gamblers, compulsive gamblers cannot walk away, even when they are losing large amounts of money. Such people's gambling progresses from an occasional pastime to an uncontrollable habit. Before gambling, compulsive gamblers are usually tense and anxious. Only by gambling do patients begin to feel better. Eventually, work, family, and social activities take a back seat to the gambling itself.

Compulsive gambling is a serious problem. It can cause financial ruin. It can even lead to criminal behaviors such as stealing, as patients try to find money to gamble with or pay off gambling debts.

According to the NIH, compulsive gambling affects as many as 3 percent of all American adults. More men than women suffer from the condition. Researchers believe that alcohol and other drug use is a risk factor for compulsive gambling.

In recent years, researchers have become more interested in compulsive gambling and how to treat it. Mental health professionals say that to deal with the condition successfully, the patient must first admit that there is a problem. Therapy and support groups can help patients learn to resist and control their urges to gamble. In addition to therapy, doctors may also prescribe antidepressants.

Kleptomania

Kleptomania (klep-toh-MAY-nee-uh) is a disorder in which people feel compelled to steal items that they do not need or want. Kleptomania is not the same as shoplifting. Some adolescents shoplift for the thrill of stealing or to defy authority. Younger children may shoplift because they don't yet understand that stealing is wrong. Adults may shoplift in order to get things that they want for nothing, even though they know that stealing is wrong. Unlike shoplifters, people with kleptomania are not able to control their impulses to steal. Before stealing, people with kleptomania feel tense and anxious. After stealing, they feel relief and pleasure.

Doctors are not sure what exactly causes kleptomania. Some researchers believe that the disorder may be related to abnormal brain chemical levels. Others believe that kleptomania may be triggered by seriously stressful events.

Women are more likely to develop this impulse-control disorder than men are. Researchers believe that kleptomania may be associated with other mental health conditions, including mood and anxiety disorders.

Kleptomania is a chronic condition that can last for years without treatment. Doctors currently treat kleptomania with a combination of therapy and medications, especially antidepressants.

Intermittent Explosive Disorder

People with *intermittent explosive disorder* can't control their tempers. A patient's frequent and unpredictable outbursts of anger are often accompanied by physical damage to people or property. In most cases, the outbursts are caused by minor incidents or stresses.

Men are more often affected by the condition than women are. Most cases occur between late adolescence and early adulthood. Some researchers believe that this condition is associated with bipolar disorder in some way. Others believe that abnormal brain chemical levels or head injuries may be a factor. Because other mental health conditions have similar symptoms, doctors must first rule out these other conditions before diagnosing intermittent explosive disorder.

Treatment for the disorder is usually a combination of therapy and medication. Antidepressants and mood stabilizers are both used to treat the disorder. However, the success of treatment for this disorder is unclear.

Pyromania

Pyromania (pye-roh-MAY-nee-uh) is a disorder in which people cannot control the impulse to set fires. As with other impulse-control disorders, people are extremely anxious and agitated before the act. After setting fires, they feel relief and pleasure. The fire is not set for profit or out of anger or revenge.

Many researchers believe that, for some people, pyromania has its roots in a childhood marked by divorce or neglect. Many

Police investigate a fatal house fire in Pennsylvania. Although people with pyromania, an impulse-control disorder, usually understand that setting fires destroys property and can threaten lives, they have no control over their actions.

people with the disorder have poor social skills and learning problems. They continue to set fires even though they understand that they are destroying property and may be putting people's lives in danger.

To be diagnosed with pyromania, people must not have any other conditions that could account for their behavior and must have set two or more fires. Therapy and medications are the usual treatments for this condition.

Trichotillomania

People with *trichotillomania* (trik-uh-til-uh-MAY-nee-uh) cannot control the impulse to tug, twist, or pull out their own hair. These actions can result in bald patches on the head, as well as a loss of eyebrows and eyelashes. As with other impulse-control disorders, people with trichotillomania feel anxiety before they begin to pull at their hair. While pulling out their hair, they experience relief and pleasure.

Doctors are not sure what causes trichotillomania. Some researchers believe that the condition may be triggered by a stressful situation at home or at school. In some people, the condition may just be a habit that becomes stronger and stronger as time goes by.

Some researchers believe that the condition may affect up to 4 percent of the U.S. population. Those most often affected by the disorder are adolescent girls. Women are four times as likely as men to suffer from this condition. The first symptoms of trichotillomania usually appear before the age of seventeen.

Small children who pull out their hair usually outgrow the condition, but if the hair pulling persists and causes noticeable hair loss, then help is needed. Hair pulling can be a symptom of some other mental health disorders. Before doctors diagnose trichotillomania, they must first eliminate other possible conditions, including mood or anxiety disorders. Trichotillomania is often treated with behavioral therapy or antidepressants.

CHAPTER 13
Sleep Disorders

Sleep disorders are conditions that interfere with a person's ability to fall asleep or stay asleep. There are more than 100 different types of sleep disorders. Some are caused by physical conditions, but others are caused by mental health problems. Sleep disorders caused by mental health conditions include insomnia, hypersomnia, and parasomnia.

Humans need sleep to restore their bodies and minds. Each night, the average human gets about 7.5 hours of sleep. During this time, the body passes through four different sleep stages. During the last two stages, the body experiences the deep sleep that is most restful.

Sleep disorders are serious problems. They can interfere with a person's ability to work and function properly during the day. People with sleep conditions may use alcohol in an attempt to make themselves sleep and feel better. However, people under the influence of alcohol usually do not enter the deep stages of sleep that are most beneficial to the body.

Insomnia

Insomnia (in-SAHM-nee-uh) is the inability to sleep. The condition is a common one, affecting as many as 30 million Americans each year. Although some cases of insomnia are caused by physical factors and conditions, about 75 percent of all cases are caused by psychological factors. Insomnia is often triggered by stress or a traumatic event. Mood disorders can also lead to insomnia.

While most people eventually overcome this condition without assistance, long-lasting insomnia can cause serious health problems. Each night before bed, a person with chronic insomnia may worry or become anxious about falling asleep. This anxiety, in turn, perpetuates the insomnia.

Insomnia is a common problem that plagues many people from time to time. Persistent insomnia, however, can have serious consequences. Lack of sleep contributes to poor health and can result in difficulties at work and school.

Symptoms of insomnia include difficulty falling asleep; waking during the night; irritability, fatigue, and a lack of concentration during the day; anxiety; and loud snoring. People who suffer from insomnia should talk to a medical professional to determine what is causing their condition. Effective treatments for chronic insomnia caused by psychological factors include behavioral therapy and medications. Tranquilizers may be prescribed if the problem is persistent and troubling.

```
┌─────────────────────────────────────────────────┐
│         Substances That Cause Insomnia            │
└─────────────────────────────────────────────────┘
```

- Caffeine

- Nicotine

- Alcohol

- Decongestants

- Asthma, thyroid, and steroid medications

Hypersomnias

Hypersomnias (hye-per-SAHM-nee-uhz) are disorders that cause a person to feel abnormally drowsy or sleepy during the day without any known physical cause. The urge to sleep may become so overwhelming that the person may nod off at inappropriate times.

One type of hypersomnia is *narcolepsy* (NAR-kuh-lep-see). A person with narcolepsy experiences sudden, frequent attacks of sleep. These attacks may occur at any time—while patients are working, driving, or in mid-conversation. Each sleep episode lasts for about fifteen minutes. After patients awake, they feel reinvigorated but may become sleepy again in just a short time.

In addition to persistent drowsiness, symptoms of narcolepsy include auditory and visual hallucinations before the sleep episode, sudden loss of muscle tone, and a temporary inability to use muscles after waking up from a sleep episode. There is no known cure for the condition, although doctors can help patients learn how to control the symptoms. In some cases, doctors may prescribe stimulants and other prescription medicines.

Parasomnias

Parasomnias (paar-uh-SAHM-nee-uhz) are abnormal behaviors that disrupt a person's sleep. These behaviors include sleepwalking, having nightmares, and experiencing night terror. These disorders, which are common in children, occur during the deepest stages of sleep.

While almost everybody has suffered from a nightmare or two, people with *nightmare disorder* experience chronic, intense nightmares that awaken them from their sleep and cause them serious distress. They can vividly recall the details of the bad dreams, and they have difficulty returning to sleep. People with this disorder may become anxious at bedtime and afraid to go to sleep.

In many cases, people begin to experience severe nightmares after a stressful or traumatic event. Children and adolescents are most likely to develop nightmare disorder. People with other mental health conditions are also at higher risk for developing this disorder.

Another type of parasomnia is *night terror*. With this disorder, a person wakes abruptly from sleep in a terrified state. Symptoms of night terror include screaming, sweating, a racing pulse, rapid breathing, and an accelerated heart rate. When others try to comfort sufferers, they are unresponsive. Unlike people with nightmare disorder, those suffering from night terror often cannot recall much of the dream that woke them. By morning, they may have forgotten the episode completely. Young boys are most at risk of developing night terror. They usually outgrow the condition without treatment. Adults who use alcohol or have extreme stress are also at a higher risk.

Doctors treat nightmare disorder and night terror with therapy and, in severe cases, with medication. They may also recommend that patients practice relaxation techniques and stress management. Hypnosis has also been used effectively to alleviate night terror.

Another type of parasomnia is *sleepwalking disorder*. People with this disorder walk or do other activities while sleeping. Sleepwalking takes place during the deepest stages of sleep. Children between the ages of six and twelve are most likely to sleepwalk. Their sleepwalking is often triggered by anxiety or fatigue. When adults walk in their sleep, however, the condition often signals other mental health problems.

Sleepwalking takes a number of different forms. Some people just sit up in bed. Others get dressed or move furniture. Sleepwalking naturally places people at an increased risk of injury as a result of tripping or losing their balance. Episodes of sleepwalking may last a few seconds or as long as thirty minutes.

When patients suffer from persistent sleepwalking episodes, doctors will examine them to make sure that they are not suffering from another medical condition. However, there is little that can be done to stop a person from sleepwalking. If a child is sleepwalking, parents may want to take extra safety precautions around the home, such as blocking off stairways. In severe cases, doctors might prescribe tranquilizers.

Fast Fact

Contrary to popular belief, it is not dangerous to awaken a sleepwalker.

CHAPTER 14
Treatments and Therapies

Most mental health disorders are treatable. In recent years, researchers have learned more about the causes and effects of such disorders as autism, schizophrenia, and other conditions. Better medications and other treatment options have improved the outlook for the millions of Americans who suffer from mental health disorders.

Treatments for mental health disorders can be separated into two general categories: psychotherapy and drug therapy. Most often, doctors will use a combination of these two types of treatment to help those suffering from mental health conditions.

Diagnosing Mental Illnesses

When someone is suffering from a mental health disorder, the first person to contact is the family doctor. The doctor will first perform a complete physical examination to rule out any other medical conditions. Then the doctor will be able to refer the patient to another professional for further tests or treatment.

The first step toward treating a mental health disorder is getting the condition properly diagnosed. Diagnosing mental health disorders is more difficult than diagnosing many physical conditions. There are no specific tests to confirm most mental illnesses, so doctors must rely on observing patients' behavior and talking to them, as well as family and friends, about their symptoms and family history. Diagnosis is made even more difficult because some symptoms are shared by a variety of different mental health conditions.

Doctors decide upon a diagnosis of a certain condition after specific criteria for that condition have been met or after a particular number of symptoms are present. In recent years, doctors have begun using *magnetic resonance imaging* (MRI) to assist them in accurately diagnosing some conditions. An MRI

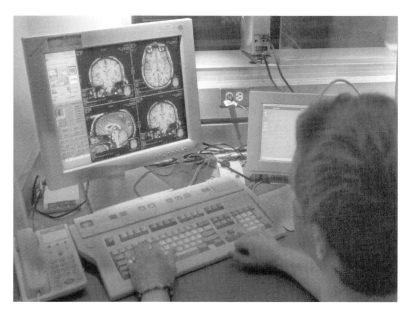

As a client's brain is scanned using magnetic resonance imaging, a graduate student at the University of Wisconsin works on a computer to project pictures for the client to view during the scan. The scan will record the client's emotional responses to the pictures, which will allow scientists to see how emotions affect the brain.

uses magnets and radio waves to create an image of the inside of the brain. Another tool that can be used is called *positron emission* (PAHZ-ih-trahn ee-MIH-shun) *tomography* (PET). A PET scan uses small amounts of radioactive substances to take pictures of the brain. These imaging techniques let researchers observe brain activity while people engage in different types of behaviors, such as one type of problem solving versus another.

Once a diagnosis has been made, the doctor and patient can begin the process of deciding which treatments will be best. The doctor may refer the patient to another mental health professional who is better suited to treat the disorder. Mental health professionals include the following:

• A *psychiatrist* (sye-KYE-uh-trist) is a medical doctor who has been specially trained to treat mental health disorders. A psychiatrist can provide psychiatric testing and evaluation, as well as psychotherapy. He or she can also write prescriptions for medications.

- A *psychologist* (sye-KAHL-oh-jist) holds a doctoral degree in clinical psychology (sye-KAHL-oh-jee) or counseling. A psychologist can provide psychological testing and evaluation, as well as psychotherapy.
- A *social worker* holds a bachelor's or master's degree in social work. A social worker can provide most forms of psychotherapy.
- A *paraprofessional* is someone who doesn't necessarily hold any degrees directly related to mental health, but who chooses to work in this field. Substance abuse counselors and pastoral counselors are paraprofessionals.

DSM

There are currently no definitive tests that can be used to diagnose mental health disorders. Instead, doctors must observe a patient's symptoms and use their knowledge to determine if the patient is suffering from a mental health problem. One important tool that doctors use in this work is a book called the *Diagnostic and Statistical Manual of Mental Disorders* (DSM). Published by the American Psychiatric Association, the DSM lists and defines all known mental and emotional disorders. To help doctors diagnose mental illness, the book includes signs and symptoms for every disorder. The fourth edition of the DSM was published in 1994, but the text was revised in 2000. The DSM-IV-TR, as it is known, lists more than 300 mental and emotional disorders that can affect people. The first edition, published in 1952, listed 106. The American Psychiatric Association expects to publish the DSM-V in 2010.

Psychotherapy

Psychotherapy (sye-koh-THERR-uh-pee) is any type of treatment that involves an exchange of words, feelings, and thoughts between a patient and a mental health professional. There are both advantages and disadvantages to psychotherapy.

Unlike drug therapy, psychotherapy has no associated physical side effects. Therapy has been shown to be very effective in easing the symptoms of anxiety and depression. However, it may take time before the benefits of psychotherapy become noticeable. Finally, psychotherapy alone is not appropriate for all types of mental health conditions.

The duration of psychotherapy varies from patient to patient. In some cases, only brief psychotherapy is needed, and the patient feels better after just a few sessions. In other cases, psychotherapy may continue for several months. According to the American Psychological Association (APA), 75 percent of all psychotherapy patients surveyed reported feeling better at the end of six months. Psychotherapy is effective for adults, children, and adolescents.

Choosing the Right Therapist

One of the most important factors in successful psychotherapy is a good therapist-patient relationship. Here are some tips from the APA on choosing the right mental health professional.

- Talk to family members and friends about their recommendations, especially if they have had good experiences with psychotherapy.
- Ask your primary care physician for a therapy referral. Explain what is important to you so that the doctor can make several good suggestions.
- Ask members of your church or synagogue to recommended therapists.
- Check the phone book for your local mental health association. This group will be able to provide a referral.
- Call and make appointments to talk to more than one therapist. These visits will help you decide which therapist is right for you.

Types of Psychotherapy

There are many different approaches to psychotherapy. Most can be categorized into one of four different groups. Most therapists combine two or more types of therapy. In the end, whatever works best for the patient should be used.

Psychodynamic Therapy and Psychoanalysis

The goal of *psychodynamic* (sye-koh-dye-NAM-ik) *therapy* is self-understanding. Together, the patient and therapist look into the person's past for clues to why the person is suffering today. Psychodynamic therapy is one of the most common types of psychotherapy.

One type of psychodynamic therapy is known as *interpersonal therapy*. During this type of therapy, patients explore their personal relations with others. The goal of interpersonal therapy is to improve relationship skills and allow patients to develop healthy relationships. This therapy has been used successfully to treat adolescent depression.

A type of therapy that is similar to psychodynamic therapy is *psychoanalysis* (sye-koh-uh-NAL-ih-siss). This type of therapy is more intensive than regular psychodynamic therapy. The patient often meets with the therapist several times a week and may continue doing so for up to six years. This type of therapy was pioneered by Sigmund Freud (froyd) (1856–1939) in the late 1890s.

Behavioral and Cognitive Therapies

The goal of these therapies is to make positive changes in a patient's behaviors, actions, and thoughts. Instead of trying to understand why a patient behaves a certain way, the therapist focuses on substituting healthy behaviors and thoughts for unhealthy ones. Part of the doctor's role in behavioral or cognitive therapy is to point the patient in the direction of useful resources.

One special field that combines behavioral and cognitive therapy is known as *cognitive-behavioral therapy*. In addition to examining unhealthy behaviors, the doctor also helps the patient explore unhealthy thinking. The goal for the patient is to replace negative thoughts (such as "I'm going to fail this test") with positive ones (such as "I know I can do this"). Cognitive-behavioral therapy has been very effective in treating children and adolescents with anxiety or depression.

Another type of behavioral therapy is *dialectical* (dye-uh-LEK-tik-ul) *behavioral therapy* (DBT). DBT encourages patients to take responsibility for their actions and explore their responses to conflict and stressful events. This type of therapy may be used to treat adolescents with suicidal thoughts or BPD.

Humanistic Therapy

Humanistic (hyoo-mun-ISS-tik) *therapy* aims to help patients understand and accept their feelings and not focus on their thoughts or behaviors. The emphasis is on the present, not the past. Once patients start to understand themselves, they can take action to change their problems.

One type of humanistic therapy is *Gestalt* (guh-SHTALT) *therapy.* This type of therapy uses role-playing and dramatization to help patients become more aware of their feelings. The emphasis is shifted away from the past and onto what is currently happening in a patient's life. The counselor helps patients by encouraging them, in a nonjudgmental way, to take responsibility for their actions.

Another type of humanistic therapy is *client-centered therapy.* In this type of treatment, the counselor is empathetic and provides unconditional support for patients. The therapist focuses on patients' abilities, as opposed to their problems.

Group Therapy

Group therapy is any therapy session that involves more than just the patient and the mental health professional. A group session usually involves as many as eight people who share a certain condition, experience, or feelings. For example, group therapy is a common way that counselors can help survivors of sexual

A group therapy session is made up of people who share similar experiences or psychological difficulties, such as these prison inmates. In the sessions, which are moderated by a mental health professional, patients gain support and a better understanding of their problems.

assault. Together, the group works with the therapist to explore feelings and develop better thought and behavior patterns. The group setting helps members realize that they are not alone. It also allows participants to develop their relationship and communication skills.

Family and couples therapy are also group therapies. *Family therapy* is often used with children or adolescents and their families—especially if the children's symptoms might stem from problems within the family. The goal of this type of therapy is to help families interact with one another in a more healthy fashion and to encourage positive, nonviolent conflict resolution.

Couples or *marriage therapy* is used to help two partners overcome their problems. The therapist may choose to meet one partner at a time or both partners at the same time. In other cases, partners may choose individual therapy, seeing two completely different therapists who may or may not talk to each other about each partner's progress.

Both family and couples therapy are usually short-term therapies. According to the American Association for Marriage and Family Therapy (AAMFT), the average length of family therapy is twelve sessions. The AAMFT also reports that marriage and family counselors treat 1.8 million people at any given time.

Play Therapy

Play therapy is a method of therapy that is often used with children between the ages of two and twelve. In play therapy, the mental health professional watches children play with blocks, dolls, puppets, drawings, and games. The therapist uses the play as an opportunity to help children recognize, express, and understand their feelings.

Hypnosis and Mental Health

Hypnosis (hip-NOH-siss) is a trancelike state of intense concentration that can be used to help some people with mental health problems. While under hypnosis, people are more open to suggestions. Some people with anxiety disorders, phobias, and substance abuse disorders have been helped with hypnosis.

Drug Therapy

Drug therapy is the use of drugs to treat mental disorders. This type of therapy is the most common type of therapy among psychiatrists, but it is not necessarily the best type of treatment for all mental disorders.

Each year, new drugs are developed that are safer and more effective than other drugs. However, children's bodies are very different from those of adults and even adolescents. Their brains and bodies are still developing, and they process medication and other substances more rapidly. Before drugs that are effective for adults can be approved for children, they must be tested extensively to make sure that they are safe and won't interfere with growth and development.

In recent years, several drugs have been tested and approved to help children with mental health conditions. Some of the most common types of drugs used to treat children and adolescents with mental health problems are the following:

Type of Drug	Conditions Treated	Side Effects
Stimulant	ADHD	Insomnia; weight loss; decreased appetite; abdominal pains; headaches
Antidepressant & antianxiety medications	Major depression; anxiety disorders; eating disorders; personality disorders; ADHD	Sedation; physical dependency
Antipsychotic medications	Schizophrenia; autism; bipolar disorder; severe conduct disorders; severe anxiety disorders	Low blood pressure; weight gain; constipation; dry mouth; blurred vision
Mood stabilizing medications & anticonvulsants	Bipolar disorder; impulse-control disorders; schizophrenia; schizoaffective disorder	Weight gain; tremors; increased urination; decreased thyroid function

Like all medications, drugs used to treat mental health disorders can cause some serious side effects. The patient, the family, and the doctor must weigh the potential benefits against the possible hazards of taking a particular medication. In fact, some drugs are approved only for certain age groups. For example, a number of antidepressant and antianxiety medications are prescribed only for people who are eighteen or older.

Is Electroconvulsive Therapy (ECT) Safe?

ECT is currently used to help people suffering from major depression who cannot take medication or who are physically unwell. It is also used to treat people with bipolar disorder and psychotic symptoms. After ECT, many people suffering from these conditions notice great improvement in their symptoms.

Some people worry that ECT is not safe. There is a slight risk of death from the procedure, and after the treatment, some people experience memory loss which can linger. Others believe that ECT can lead to permanent brain damage.

Treatment Programs

When patients have serious mental health conditions, they may need to take part in intensive treatment programs. These treatment programs will include therapy and in some cases, will include medication.

Outpatient programs are treatment programs that do not require patients to be hospitalized. These programs are the most common type of treatment for mental health disorders. Outpatient programs can take place at a therapist's office, at a clinic or hospital, at school or home, or at a quiet meeting place where the patient can speak freely.

Another type of program is called *day treatment* or *partial hospitalization*. In recent years, the number of youths in day treatment programs has grown. A patient who takes part in this type of program spends the day at a hospital or clinic and then returns home for the night. Day treatment is more intensive than outpatient treatment. However, it allows the patient to still have the support of friends and family. Children with disruptive disorders have been effectively treated with such programs.

In cases of severe mental health disorders, a person may be placed in an *inpatient program*. With this type of treatment, the patient is confined to a hospital, treatment center, or psychiatric facility. The patient is unable to leave until the treatment is finished. The average length of stay in an inpatient program is twelve days.

The decision to place a person in an inpatient program is not taken lightly. For some children with severe mental health disorders, however, inpatient treatment is necessary. For example, children and adolescents with substance abuse disorders, eating disorders, or major depression may need to be hospitalized for their own safety.

Complementary or Alternative Therapies

In addition to psychotherapy and drug therapy, there are other types of treatments that some people choose to try. Most of these therapies are used in conjunction with more traditional psychotherapies or drug therapies.

One type of treatment is known as *expressive therapy*. Expressive therapy uses music, dance, and art to help people express their feelings and emotions. It is often used with people who suffer from schizophrenia and other conditions.

Eye movement desensitization and reprocessing (EMDR) is a type of therapy that uses rapid eye movements, hand claps, and sounds to help patients suffering from some mental health disorders. Some believe that these techniques stimulate the brain and free trapped memories, allowing people to better process and handle traumatic events. EMDR has been used extensively with people suffering from PTSD. Although some people say that EMDR has helped them through major depression and other mood disorders, there is no hard evidence to support its effectiveness.

Biofeedback is a treatment that uses electrodes and visual or auditory displays to help people learn to control their bodies' responses to stressful events. Biofeedback teaches people how to lower blood pressure, reduce muscle tension, slow breathing, and lower skin temperature. These are all signs of calmness and relaxation.

According to the NIMH, a healthy lifestyle may improve the effectiveness of any type of therapy. Healthy habits include cutting caffeine out of the diet, taking part in aerobic exercise, and avoiding illegal drug use. The NIMH also states that meditation may help, but that there is no hard evidence yet to definitively support its use.

Dorothea Dix, Mental Health Crusader

In 1841, a teacher named Dorothea Dix (1802–1887) volunteered to teach a Sunday school class for female prisoners in a Massachusetts prison. At the prison, Dix was horrified to find mentally ill women living in dirty, unhealthy conditions. She lobbied the courts to install stoves for warmth and renovate the prison, which they eventually did.

Dix began researching the state of mental health care around the nation. She soon learned that in asylums across the United States, the mentally ill were being starved, beaten, chained to walls, or locked into small closets.

For the rest of her life, Dix focused her efforts on improving the care for people with mental health conditions. Dix traveled the country, speaking about the importance of treating the mentally ill kindly and humanely. As a result of her efforts, thirty-two states built new hospitals or improved existing ones to treat the mentally ill.

CHAPTER 15
Managing Mental Health

Good mental health is an important part of achieving overall wellness. *Wellness* is the condition of being in top shape emotionally, intellectually, physically, and socially. Managing your mental health is just as important as keeping physically fit. There are things that you can do to stay as mentally healthy as possible.

What does being mentally healthy mean? It means that you are in control of your thoughts, feelings, and behavior. You are able to handle most situations when they come your way. Although it's normal to lose your cool once in a while, it shouldn't become a pattern.

Control Your Anger

Anger is a normal emotion. Depending upon how anger is handled, it can be positive or negative. Sometimes, anger encourages people to change things in their lives that are unfair or unhealthy. However, when people let angry emotions take control, anger can be a very dangerous and damaging emotion.

The first step in dealing with anger is to recognize and identify angry feelings. Put these angry feelings into words. Make sure that you know exactly who or what you are angry at and why you are angry.

Although angry feelings are normal, it's important not to act when you are maddest. Anger can cloud thinking. First, try to get rid of the anger by taking a break and walking away. You can come back to the problem later and try to resolve it. If you can't walk away, take a deep breath and count to ten before you speak. Another way to handle anger is to find something funny to laugh at. Humor is a great way to deflect angry feelings and make yourself—and others—feel better.

Focus on the Positive

Sometimes, it seems as if everything in the world is going wrong. You failed a math test, your mom is upset with you, and it's supposed to rain all weekend long. At times like this, it's especially important to focus on the good things in your life.

Positive thinking is an important part of maintaining mental wellness. Positive thinking means focusing on the good things around you. Even the smallest things might lift your mood a little.

Negative thoughts can really bring you down. One way to get rid of negative thoughts is to imagine these thoughts written in sand near the ocean. Then visualize a wave washing over them and erasing them forever.

Talk It Out

One of the best things that you can do for your mental health is to learn to express your emotions and feelings in a positive way. Learn how to share your feelings with someone that you trust. This person might be a friend, a family member, or a trusted adult.

When you have more serious problems and you can't talk to your friends and family members, there are other adults who will be willing to lend an ear. These adults include a pastor or rabbi, a school guidance counselor, a therapist, or a teacher. Don't keep your troubles inside!

Get Physical

Everyone knows that exercise helps keep the body fit. Recent studies have also shown a strong link between staying active and improved mental health. The benefits of exercise and sports include decreased depression and anxiety, better moods, and an improved sense of well-being and confidence.

Having a healthy diet is another way to make sure that your body and mind are well cared for. A healthy diet is low in fat

Being physically active is one of the best ways to maintain mental health, and establishing an active lifestyle early on helps ensure good fitness habits for life. Here, an instructor leads an aerobics class at a kids-only health club in Chicago.

and contains plenty of grains, vegetables, and fruits. Doctors also recommend avoiding too much salt, sugar, and caffeine.

Another important part of maintaining mental wellness is avoiding harmful substances. Tobacco products, alcohol, and illegal drugs have all been shown to have negative effects on mental health. They can also have serious effects on your physical well-being.

Reduce the Stress

Stress is not necessarily a bad thing. It can be a positive force, motivating people to do their best. Too much stress, however, can cause both mental and physical problems. One way to reduce stress is to avoid taking on more than you can handle. Recognize when you're overwhelmed, and don't be afraid to say no.

There are a number of relaxation exercises that people can do to help them calm down and chill out. These exercises include sitting quietly (meditation), deep breathing, and going for a quiet walk. There are many other ways to relax, as well, such as playing sports, listening to music, and gardening.

Other Ways to Foster Mental Health

Here are some more tips for keeping mentally healthy.

- Take part in after-school activities or sign up for volunteer work. They can help boost self-confidence, self-esteem, and mental wellness.

- Expect great things from yourself. Don't settle for average effort—always try to do your best.

- Get plenty of sleep. Sleep restores both the mind and the body.

- Know what works best for you. If waiting until late at night to do your homework stresses you out, try to avoid doing this. If you prefer waiting to talk to your parents after you've had half an hour after school to chill out, let them know.

- Keep a journal. Writing down your thoughts and feelings can help you identify and understand things that anger or upset you.

- Give yourself a break. Take some time each day to do something that you enjoy. Read the comics page, listen to a CD, or shoot some hoops. Reward yourself.

When Nothing Works

It's normal to feel sad, lonely, or unwanted at times. Everyone has bad days. However, when these bad days stretch into weeks and months, and when nothing seems to make you feel better, it's time to ask for help.

Mental health problems can affect anyone. In fact, mental health conditions in children are not uncommon. According to the Federation of Families for Children's Mental Health (FFCMH), between 6 million and 8 million children have a mental, emotional, or behavioral disorder that needs treatment. That's about 12 percent of the U.S. population of children. Half of these children have problems that are severe and persistent.

Mental health problems, like physical conditions, can be treated. One of the most important things that parents can do for children is to seek a doctor's help if they suspect their children are suffering from depression, anxiety, substance abuse, or any other mental health conditions. Additionally, one of the most important things that you can do for yourself is to ask for help. Talk to a family member, teacher, guidance counselor, or other trusted adult. It could be the first step to feeling better.

Timeline of Psychology

This section presents a timeline of key events in psychology.

DATE	EVENT
Late fifth century to early fourth century B.C.E.	Ancient Greek philosophers Socrates (c.469–399 B.C.E.), Plato (c.428–c.347 B.C.E.), and Aristotle (384–322 B.C.E.) teach and write about how humans learn and why people experience the world in different ways. They also wrestle with ethical questions in hopes of understanding human nature. Aristotle writes the first book on psychology as a separate topic from the rest of philosophy, titled *Para Psyche*.
	The Greek physician Hippocrates (c.460–c.377 B.C.E.), called the father of medicine, proposes that all diseases have natural—not magical—causes.
1247	The world's first mental hospital, Saint Mary of Bethlehem, opens in London, England.
1649	French philosopher René Descartes (1596–1650) proposes that all mental ability originates in the *pineal gland,* located in the brain. According to his concept of *interactive dualism,* the body can be studied scientifically, but the mind defies scientific analysis.
late 1600s	Two English philosophers, Thomas Hobbes (1588–1679) and John Locke (1632–1704), disagree with Descartes's concept of dualism. Their view, that the mind and the body are one, becomes known as *monism.*
1808	German physician Franz Joseph Gall (1758–1828) proposes that the size and shape of the skull reveal information about an individual's personality.
1855	The New York State Lunatic Asylum for Insane Convicts—the world's first mental hospital for criminal patients separate from a prison or general hospital—opens in Auburn, New York.
1859	English biologist Charles Darwin (1809–1882) publishes *On the Origin of Species by Means of Natural Selection.* Darwin's work has a profound influence on William James, one of the founders of modern psychology.

1872   Darwin publishes *The Expression of the Emotions in Man and Animals.*

1875   William James (1842–1910), a professor at Harvard University, teaches the first college course in psychology.

1879   Wilhelm Wundt (1832–1920), pictured, founds the world's first formal laboratory of psychology at the University of Leipzig, Germany.

1883   G. Stanley Hall (1844–1924) establishes the first laboratory of psychology in the United States at Johns Hopkins University in Maryland.

1885   Hermann Ebbinghaus (1850–1909) publishes *Memory: A Contribution to Experimental Psychology.*

1886   Sigmund Freud (1856–1939) begins treating psychiatric patients in Vienna, Austria, marking the beginning of personality theory.

1890   James publishes a two-volume book, *Principles of Psychology,* which combines his theories on psychology and philosophy with autobiographical tales. Influenced by Darwin, James proposes a view of psychology that later becomes known as *functionalism.*

                New York State passes the State Care Act, which orders mentally ill patients out of poorhouses and into state hospitals for treatment, and creates the first institution in the United States for psychiatric research for mental disorders.

1892   The American Psychological Association (APA) is founded.

1896   The first psychological clinic is developed at the University of Pennsylvania, marking the birth of clinical psychology.

1900   Freud publishes *The Interpretation of Dreams.* He regards dreams as valuable windows into the unconscious mind.

1905   In France, psychologist Alfred Binet (1857–1911) publishes *New Methods for the Diagnosis of the Intellectual Level of Subnormals*, in which he describes how he developed the first intelligence tests.

Mary Whiton Calkins (1863–1930) becomes the first woman president of the APA. She had studied psychology at Harvard University with William James in the late 1800s.

1906   *The Journal of Abnormal Psychology* is founded by Morton Prince (1854–1929).

Ivan Pavlov (1849–1936), pictured, studies the digestive system in dogs and makes observations that lead to his well-known findings about a basic kind of learning known as *classical conditioning.*

1911   Alfred Adler (1870–1937) leaves Freud's psychoanalytic group to form his own school of thought. Adler proposes a theory that stresses the influences of childhood.

Edward Thorndike (1874–1949) publishes the first article on animal intelligence. Inspired by Thorndike's research, behaviorist B.F. Skinner (1904–1990) later develops the theory of *operant conditioning.*

1912   William Stern (1871–1938) develops the original formula for the intelligence quotient (IQ) after studying the scores on Binet's intelligence test.

Max Wertheimer (1880–1943) publishes research on the perception of movement, which marks the beginning of Gestalt psychology.

1913   John B. Watson (1878–1958) publishes *Psychology as a Behaviorist Views It,* marking the beginning of behavioral psychology.

Citing Freud's inability to acknowledge religion and spirituality in the study of the mind, psychiatrist Carl Jung (1875–1961) starts to develop his own theories of psychology.

1916	Psychologist Lewis Terman (1877–1956) adapts Binet's intelligence test for U.S. schoolchildren and publishes the Stanford-Binet Intelligence Scale.
1917	Robert Yerkes (1876–1956), the president of the APA, develops the army Alpha and Beta Tests to measure intelligence in a group format.
1938	Skinner publishes *The Behavior of the Organisms.*
1942	Carl Rogers (1902–1987) publishes *Counseling and Psychotherapy,* which proposes to therapists that a respectful, nonjudgmental approach to clients (patients) is the key to the effective treatment of mental health problems.

Jean Piaget (1896–1980) publishes *The Psychology of Intelligence,* which discusses his theories of cognitive development.

The Minnesota Multiphasic Personality Inventory (MMPI) is developed and fast becomes the most widely researched and accepted psychological assessment device.

1952	Hans Eysenck (1916–1997), pictured, publishes a controversial study on the effectiveness of psychotherapy. His research suggests that therapy is no more effective than no treatment at all.

The first edition of the *Diagnostic and Statistical Manual of Mental Disorders* (DSM) is published by the American Psychiatric Association, marking the beginning of modern classification of mental illness.

Thorazine is first used in the treatment of schizophrenia, marking the first biochemical approach to treating mental illness.

1953	The Code of Ethics for Psychologists is developed by the APA.

The American Cancer Society (ACS) reports that cancer causes death more quickly in patients with repressed personalities. This sparks more research on how cancer patients use stress management strategies to cope with their condition.

1954   Humanist psychologist Abraham Maslow (1908-1970) publishes
            Motivation and Personality, which includes his hierarchy of needs.
            This theory describes human motivation in terms of lower needs
            and higher needs. In order for people to pursue higher needs,
            such as the need to satisfy their curiosity, they must first take care
            of the lower needs, such as food and safety.

1956   Solomon Asch (1907–1996) publishes his studies about conformity.

1964   Stanley Milgram (1933–1984) publishes *Obedience to Authority.*

1967   Aaron Beck (1921–) publishes a psychological model of
            depression suggesting that thoughts play a significant role in the
            development and maintenance of depression.

1983   Howard Gardner (1943–) introduces his theory of multiple
            intelligences. This theory argues that the concept of intelligence
            should be used to improve lives, not to measure and quantify
            human beings.

1997   IBM's supercomputer Deep Blue beats the world's best chess
            player, Garry Kasparov (1963–), marking a milestone in the
            development of artificial intelligence.

1998   Psychology advances to the technological age with the emergence
            of *e-therapy,* psychotherapy via the Internet.

2003   In a rematch, Kasparov plays
            chess against an IBM computer
            known as Deep Junior. In the
            six-game match, Kasparov wins
            once, the computer wins once,
            and they tie four times.

            Scientists at the Human Genome Project complete their mission
            to identify the 3.1 billion units that make up human DNA. The
            more that scientists know about the human genome, the more
            they will be able to understand how mental disorders are inherited
            and how they might be treated.

Glossary

adolescence—the stage of a person's development that begins with puberty and continues through the teen years until adulthood

anxiety—nervousness and panic caused by a feeling of uncertainty or danger

behavior—any observable action of a person or animal (some psychologists include thoughts and emotions as behaviors, as well)

behavioral psychology—the scientific study of the ways that people learn, with an emphasis on how rewards and punishment in the environment affect behavior; sometimes called behaviorism

central nervous system—the brain and spinal cord

cognition—how the mind works: how it thinks, learns, memorizes, solves problems, imagines, and more

cognitive psychology—the branch of psychology that focuses on the scientific study of the mind, exploring mental activities such as sensation, perception, motor control, attention, memory, learning, language, reasoning, problem solving, and decision making

delusion—a persistent belief that is strongly held despite evidence that the belief is actually false

depression—a mood disorder that involves extended periods of feeling deep sadness, hopelessness, and worthlessness

environment—the conditions that surround an organism as it grows; these can include climate, nutrition, other living things, and anything else that affects development

experiment—a procedure in which a researcher systematically arranges conditions in order to find out what will happen

genetics—the study of heredity and how characteristics are passed from parent to child

hallucination—a symptom of a variety of severe mental disorders which involves a false or distorted perception of objects or events

humanistic psychology—the branch of psychology that emphasizes the human capacity for growth and choice

paranoia—an intense worry that others are out to hurt someone, even though there is no real evidence to support this belief

perception—the process of interpreting information that is received through the senses

personality—a person's consistent pattern of thinking, feeling, and acting

phobia—an intense, irrational fear caused by an object, situation, or person

psychiatry—the study of psychology with an emphasis on biological factors

psychoanalysis—the theory and method of therapy developed and practiced by Sigmund Freud in the early 1900s

psychodynamic theory—the branch of psychology that emphasizes the role of the unconscious mind in shaping personality and influencing behavior

psychology—the scientific study of how people think, feel, and behave

psychosis—a severe mental disorder in which a person loses touch with reality and experiences distorted thoughts, perceptions, and emotions

psychotherapy—the treatment of a mental, emotional, or social disorder by a psychiatrist, psychologist, or counselor

schizophrenia—a severe mental disorder in which a person has a breakdown in perceptual and thought processes, often experiencing hallucinations and delusions

stress—the physical and psychological result of internal or external pressure

Bibliography

Books

American Psychiatric Association. *Diagnostic and Statistical Manual of Mental Disorders, Text Revision (DSM-IV-TR)*. Washington, DC: American Psychiatric Press, 2000.

Bellenir, Karen, ed. *Mental Health Information for Teens.* Detroit: Omnigraphics, 2001.

Cobain, Bev. *When Nothing Matters Anymore: A Survival Guide for Depressed Teens.* Minneapolis: Free Spirit Publishing, 1998.

Kent, Deborah. *Snake Pits, Talking Cures, and Magic Bullets: A History of Mental Illness.* Brookfield, CT: Twenty-First Century Books, 2003.

Mitchell, Hayley R. *Teen Suicide.* San Diego: Lucent Books, 2000.

Philips, Jane E. *Schizophrenia.* Berkeley Heights, NJ: Enslow Publishers, 2003.

Waltz, Mitzi. *Bipolar Disorder: A Guide to Helping Children and Adolescents.* Sebastopol, CA: O'Reilly, 2000.

Web Sites

American Academy of Child and Adolescent Psychiatry (AACAP) *www.aacap.org*

American Psychological Association (APA) *www.apa.org*

National Eating Disorders Association (NEDA) *www.nationaleatingdisorders.org*

United States Department of Health and Human Services Substance Abuse and Mental Health Services Administration (SAMHSA) *www.mentalhealth.org*

Index

Note: Page numbers in *italics* indicate illustrations and captions.